The Path to PERFECT FREEDOM

Shyalpa Tenzin Rinpoche

Light of Wisdom

Light of Wisdom Publications
335 East 14th Street, Unit 1584, New York, NY 10009

ISBN - 979-8-218-91060-0

CONTENTS

PART THREE · KEY TOPICS

APPENDIX

EDITOR'S FOREWORD

His Eminence Shyalpa Tenzin Rinpoche often says that breathing easily in a relaxed state free from stress and worry is a sign of inner freedom. Since time without beginning, our true nature has been, is, and always will be, naturally free.

The great omniscient Longchenpa wrote, "The ultimate nature of all beings is the perfect state of enlightenment. Knowing this to be true, I commit to supreme realization."

This is the path of Dzogchen, the Great Perfection. It begins with the hinayana vehicle, the path of individual liberation, then progresses to the mahayana with the vow to seek enlightenment for the benefit of all sentient beings, and culminates in the path of vajrayana and Dzogchen—the highest path to ultimate freedom.

This book presents a collection of teachings by His Eminence Shyalpa Tenzin Rinpoche, delivered across the United States and Asia over the past 35 years. It highlights Rinpoche's direct, spontaneous, and engaging style.

Part One features general teachings on the Tibetan Buddhist path. These talks cover topics such as the purity of being, the essence of wisdom, the infallible law of karma, unconditional intelligence, pure aspiration, and the way of the bodhisattva.

Part Two focuses on the teachings of the vajrayana and Dzogchen. It begins with a line-by-line commentary on His Holiness Dudjom Rinpoche's *Calling the Lama from Afar*, and a talk on devotion within the lineage of Padmasambhava. It includes Rinpoche's teachings on the five extraordinary preliminary practices of the *Pema Sangtig Ngondro*: taking refuge, generating bodhichitta, Vajrasattva purification, mandala offering, and Guru Yoga, followed by a review and commentary on His Holiness Dudjom Rinpoche's *Quintessence of Accomplishment: Instructions for Mountain Retreat.* It concludes with an exploration of Patrul Rinpoche's teachings on *The Inner Treasure of Self-Liberation.*

Part Three, Key Topics, includes a selection of short teachings on specific subjects, such as "The Kindness of the Teacher," "Beyond Death," and "Unborn Awareness." Rinpoche delivered many of these teachings in response to students' questions.

These teachings were compiled from transcripts and audio recordings. I wish to express my thanks to Sam Fohr and Dan Bernatowicz for recording many of these teachings, and Dan for converting them to digital format. Also, thank you to Pema Tara for her careful work on transcription. A special thanks to Philip Smith for his thorough and diligent copyediting.

Above all, I thank my principal teacher, His Eminence Kyabje Shyalpa Tenzin Rinpoche, for his compassionate guidance and wisdom, and for this invaluable gem of teachings. May all who seek inner freedom and lasting fulfillment benefit from them.

Paul J. Patrick, editor

Having realized that both subject and object are of the nature of space—having never existed—one experiences all phenomena within a state of perfect freedom.

— Longchenpa

Buddha Shakyamuni

PART ONE
PUBLIC TALKS

THE PURITY OF BEING

The spiritual path is accessible to everyone, believers and non-believers alike. Moreover, living a spiritual life is essential; we cannot afford to be without it. Contrived ideas about purity can be fabricated with clever philosophy, but this is not true spirituality. We must recognize that our true nature is *inherently pure and unconditioned*. If your true nature were not pure from the beginning, you could not make it pure. We must always question religious beliefs and dogma, which often suggest that our original nature is somehow flawed. Many people seek a savior outside themselves when they lack confidence in the inherently pure essence of their being.

Consider the possibility that the nature of your mind is perfect just as it is. When you overthink and conceptualize, you obscure this natural purity and burden yourself with unnecessary thoughts and distractions. The mind is inherently pure from the start, so you don't need to look for this perfection elsewhere. It resides within us all.

When you recognize this purity, you feel joy and fulfillment. Working in the office, caring for your children, getting sick, or mourning the death of a loved one—they are all active expressions of unobstructed energy—in essence, the purity of your being. Therefore, you are fully aware and fully alive, in whatever way the energy manifests. Ordinarily, we miss this pure expression in our daily lives.

We tend to identify with our self-concepts, which obscure our true nature. But the essence of our being is not subject to movement or change. It is primordially pure and unchanging. Genuine confidence comes when you recognize this universal truth.

•••

Question: How do we cultivate this fundamental purity?

Rinpoche: Your original nature is like a diamond; it has always been pure. There has never been a moment when it was impure. You recognize this nature, which is like the immutable purity of the diamond. This purity is always there within, but you have to actualize and experience it.

Could your essence be made white if it were black as coal? If your nature were not originally pure, no amount of cultivation could make it so.

If your nature is primordially pure, how could you cultivate it? Is it possible? Is it necessary? This is why I say that a life of pure spirituality is indispensable. Yes, our nature is pure, but is this purity experienced now in our day-to-day lives?

For this purity to become the wholeness of your life, you need to awaken great trust in your true nature and strong determination now, in this very moment. A spiritual path will empower you to be yourself, to recognize and remain in your natural state. What could be better than this? What else would we need beyond this? Sadly, without this trust and confidence, we feel impoverished and discontented. In the purity of being, we find joy in every breath, and this alone will be more than enough.

We need to keep things simple. We must see each other honestly and accept everyone's vulnerabilities and weaknesses, including our own. Seeing others through the clear eyes of compassion and understanding, we can live fully and treasure this most precious human life.

EVERY DAY IS AN AUSPICIOUS DAY

On our Himalayan Buddhist calendars, we have many special auspicious days. However, for the Buddhist practitioner, every day can be auspicious. Each day, we have the opportunity to realize the essence of our being. Every moment offers us the chance to awaken. From this point of view, every day is precious.

In a sense, you are only one moment away from attaining enlightenment. If you continue to miss this moment, it may not arise again for many lifetimes. Therefore, after obtaining a precious human life, if you meet a compassionate teacher and wholeheartedly immerse your body, speech, and mind in following a spiritual path, you have the potential to actualize liberation from suffering cyclic existence in this very lifetime. This indestructible path can guide you clearly and directly. Thus, you are fortunate to follow this profound path, absorb these teachings, and discover the ultimate, unconditional awakening.

Recognizing that life is precious, we must embrace compassion and loving-kindness for all sentient beings, as everyone deserves our compassion and understanding.

Every individual is on the way to enlightenment. However, our true nature is obscured, and because of this, we suffer. Lacking compassion and understanding, we fail to uplift ourselves. With compassion, we demonstrate intelligence and integrity. As you observe your friends and foes, recognize their deepest longing to be free from suffering and find true happiness and freedom.

If there are disagreements, it indicates that we are not seeing the whole picture. Confusion only leads to disputes. Therefore, we must give each other space. We should also allow space for our thoughts. In other words, when a thought arises, let it be; don't follow the first thought with a second thought, and so on. This space gives rise to clarity. We relax in this space and see the natural perfection in each moment.

This is where you foster respect for others and see the beauty in simply being yourself. All spiritual practice must be grounded in this natural purity. The greatest gift you can offer is the gift of clarity and understanding.

Find clarity in the space between thoughts. The accomplished masters have all the space they need, as they are integrated with the space of awareness. In the Guru's presence, everything feels right. You may have many questions, doubts, and chaos in your life. But in the master's presence, it all dissolves and feels magical. You feel at ease and satisfied, even if the Guru has nothing special to offer you.

As a practitioner, you need to see the actual cause of your suffering. The luminous path of Dzogchen reveals the root of all happiness and misery. This is exactly what we need. There's no time to beat around the bush, so to speak. On this path, you don't fool around; you get straight to the point, understanding that your time in this form is limited. The air you're breathing could be taken from you at any moment.

The most meaningful thing is to be a friend to yourself and realize what is significant in this very moment, in this very lifetime.

We should practice and follow the path of Dharma as if there were no tomorrow. When you smile, do so sincerely, as if it were your last chance. When you give a gift to your friend, offer it as if it were your final opportunity. Show your respect and devotion to your teacher, recognizing that time and circumstance are uncertain. When enjoying your lunch, savor your meal, for it could be your last. In this way, all your actions are spontaneously accomplished.

Merely receiving the refuge vow from the Guru is insufficient. When you take refuge, you commit to following the Buddha, Dharma, and Sangha. Following the Three Jewels is having a warm, compassionate heart—a boundless heart. You pledge to awaken from the slumber of ignorance.

Today, we will have a *ganachakra* feast offering. A feast offering is a celebration in which we express our appreciation and recognize our opportunities and our potential for enlightenment. You celebrate because you know you have everything you need to be your true self. Whether or not there is a next moment, you celebrate by living fully in *this* moment.

Indeed, everything is a feast and an offering. Your body is worth offering, your speech is worth offering, and your mind is worth offering. The whole universe is worth offering. All the fruits and flowers, all the mountains and rivers—they are all worthy of offering. You lack nothing. When you feel you lack nothing, that feeling itself is an offering. That feeling flows through your veins, opening you up to give and receive. You can rest at ease and be free from conditional attachments. When we celebrate this profound practice with like-minded individuals who share our *samaya* and understand the teachings and the teacher, we witness its beauty; it rejuvenates us and benefits all sentient beings.

ESSENCE OF WISDOM

When we indulge in our desires and cravings, we might feel we are living fully. But with craving and attachment, we waste our precious human lives, endlessly searching for something better, something more. This way of distraction lacks true freedom.

We laugh out of ignorance, and we chatter to distract ourselves. Everything we seem to enjoy is temporary and doesn't last. If we are slaves to our desires, a beautiful home, gracious friends, and sumptuous food will not bring any genuine fulfillment. We grow attached to what is fleeting, transient, and dreamlike. The seemingly beautiful things aren't the truly beautiful things, and we fail to see that they rob us of our freedom.

One moment, we feel happy, and the next, we feel sad. One moment, we are up, and the next, we are down. This is like a big joke, a grand illusion. We grow tired and restless without realizing that we're getting closer and closer to our last breath. We are like children, busy building fabulous sandcastles on the beach. But soon, the waves will wash them all away.

How freeing it is to be in the timeless moment, without holding onto thoughts of past, present, or future. Within this expansive space, nothing can take away our freedom. How fulfilling this moment is! In this timeless awareness of nowness, everything naturally arises and naturally dissolves.

The essence of our being is pure, like a clear sky free of clouds. Yet we are lost in a fog of thoughts, not realizing our mirror-like essence is unstained. When we do not recognize the purity of this essence, we identify with and judge what appears in the mirror. But this unconditional essence has no judgment whatsoever. Who judges your strengths and your weaknesses? How freeing it is—to know that this mirror-like essence is free of all judgment.

What are we chasing, and why are we running around in circles when nothing can be accomplished in this contrived way? Complete fulfillment is found effortlessly in the essence of our being. This complete perfection is within our reach! It has never been apart from us. It is so close to us, but we are blind and cannot see it. It is time to recognize our true nature!

On the path to freedom, we purify and burn up the conditioning of karma. The effects of karma are created when we are not dwelling in our natural essence, the state of complete freedom. Without true freedom, we are entangled in conflicting thoughts and disturbing emotions. We chase after illusory dreams and lustful desires, which is like chasing a mirage to quench our thirst. We don't recognize the ungraspable, rainbow-like nature of our aimless dreams and desires.

Perfect freedom is free from the conditioned past, present, and future. In this state of unconditional essence, there is complete openness where anything is possible. This might threaten the fragile ego, which is unfamiliar with the vastness of natural wisdom. But there is no other way except this sublime path of total awareness—the openness where everything is possible.

When we fail to actualize this pure wisdom energy, we have no control over what may happen next. Therefore, relax, rest, and be fearlessly open in every situation. Whatever happens, feel it and experience it to the fullest. Live this life fully by remembering that the end of life is possible at any given moment. This is the most intelligent way of being. This is my humble advice. Please take it to heart.

Realize that the nature of your mind is none other than your teacher's wisdom mind. Then, you and the teacher are inseparable in a state of great equanimity. Then, the Lama is always in your heart, and the essence of wisdom is within you.

THE FOUR POINTS THAT TURN THE MIND TO DHARMA

The General Preliminaries of the Pema Sangtig Ngondro

This birth, endowed with the eight freedoms and ten favorable conditions
Is like the Udambara flower, hard to find again and again.
Once attained, its great potential is equal to a wish-fulfilling jewel.
Please bless me so that I may realize the essence of this precious life.

The outer world is impermanent, subject to destruction by water or fire.
Its inner inhabitants, the lives of sentient beings are not permanent,
Even for a moment, reaching closer and closer to death.
Please bless me to take to heart the meaning of death.

When death comes, following the results of positive and negative karma,
Virtue leads to bliss and non-virtue brings suffering states.
The result of karma is infallible; therefore,
Please bless me to be able to accept virtue and reject non-virtue.

Wherever one is born, in higher or lower parts of the
three realms,
Since one is constantly miserable from the three types
of suffering,
With the intention to completely renounce samsara,
I shall meditate on the profound yoga of the supreme path!

•••

In Tibetan Buddhism, the general preliminaries are called *lo dok nam zhi,* which refers to the four points that turn the mind toward Dharma. The first point is obtaining a precious human birth. What are the qualities that make this human birth so precious? It says in the *sadhana* text: "This birth, endowed with the eight freedoms and ten favorab le conditions, is like the Udumbara flower, hard to find again and again." This precious human life is rare and not easy to attain. When a buddha appears in our eon, an Udumbara flower appears. The Udumbara flower is a symbol of something very precious and very difficult to find. When you have this precious human existence, you are incredibly fortunate. Therefore, you pray to the Lama to make the most of this precious human life.

Now, what are the qualities that make this human life precious? A precious life is endowed with eight freedoms and ten favorable conditions. Five of the ten favorable conditions are personal:

1. You are born as a human
2. You are born in a land where there is teaching of Dharma
3. You are born with all sense faculties intact
4. You have an honest and positive vocation
5. You have interest and faith in the Dharma.

The other five are circumstantial conditions:

1. You are born in a bright eon where a buddha has appeared
2. You are born in an eon where a buddha has taught the Dharma
3. You are born where the teachings of Dharma endure
4. You are born where the teachings of Dharma are followed
5. You are born where great beings teach out of love and compassion for others.

The eight freedoms are freedom from states where there is no opportunity to practice the Dharma:

1. in a hell realm
2. in a hungry ghost realm
3. in the animal realm
4. as a long-living god realm
5. born in uncivilized lands
6. with incomplete faculties
7. having wrong views
8. being in a time when no Buddha has appeared.

When you have attained this precious human life with these endowments, use them wisely. It is hard to obtain all the freedoms and favorable conditions. Therefore, when you have them, you must practice the pure Dharma from the bottom of your heart.

To understand how difficult it is to obtain these conditions, we have the example of a blind turtle that surfaces in the ocean only once every one hundred years. Now, floating on the surface of this ocean is a single yoke used for harnessing cattle for work in the fields. The wind is blowing the yoke back and forth. At any given moment, there is no predicting where the yoke might be or where in the great ocean the turtle will surface. How unlikely it would be for the blind turtle to find its head in the yoke! The yoke represents this precious human body, and the wind is one's karma, blowing the yoke over the vast ocean of existence. It is harder to achieve a precious human birth than for the blind turtle to slip its head into the yoke. Having the extremely good fortune to be born as a human with the ten favorable conditions and eight freedoms is extremely rare! Therefore, we must always try to understand and actualize the essence of a precious human birth.

The second point is the reality of impermanence and death. Both the material world and the world of sentient beings are transient. The outer world is not permanent; it could be destroyed by fire, flood, volcano, etc. The inhabitants of this world, all sentient beings, are also impermanent. Today, birth might take place. Tomorrow, death might occur. There is no certainty that you will live for even one more day. Every moment brings one closer and closer to death. Always remember the truth of impermanence and the certainty of death.

Your precious human life is like a lamp lighting your way on a dark road. Imagine that the road is filled with poisonous snakes and vicious animals. A terrible storm is raging, and your lamp could be extinguished at any moment. Left in the dark, you would be helpless, not knowing where to turn.

So, what now? You have obtained this human body. You have received the teachings. You have the blessings of a compassionate teacher. Do you want to live more fully, with liberation from suffering, or do you want to have more insecurity and less capacity to deal with change and uncertainty? You can handle changing circumstances most effectively by realizing the truth of impermanence. You can recognize impermanence by observing both the external changes in the world and the internal changes in your body, speech, and mind. Remarkably, these elements change so quickly! This is the essence of impermanence.

The third point is the inevitability of karma. You will find that creating good karma brings positive results. Creating bad karma brings negative results. If you cultivate greed, there is more suffering; if you cultivate generosity, there is more contentment and happiness. If you cultivate anger, there is more suffering; if you practice patience, there is more happiness. If you practice mindfulness, you make fewer mistakes; if you act ignorantly, you make more conflict. This is the third point that turns the mind to Dharma: the infallible nature of karma, cause and effect.

If you can handle the changes in your life, you will be able to handle the inevitability of death. If you have the intelligence to take care of your life, when death arrives before you, you will have nothing to regret or fear. If you spend your whole life chasing worldly accomplishments and accumulating more and more mundane possessions, when death comes, you will still not have finished accumulating. There will be so much more left for you to achieve.

Don't allow yourself to indulge in negativity, not even for a single moment. Embrace all that is positive. When you feel anger, arrogance, greed, or jealousy, nip it in the bud. Be aware of your own faults, and always see the goodness in others.

So, with a deep understanding of cause and effect, you should pray like this: *"By having complete confidence in the infallibility of cause and effect, may I know how to abandon wrongdoing. May I know how to accumulate merit and foster the causes that bring favorable results."*

The defects and repulsive nature of samsara are the fourth of the four points that turn one's mind toward Dharma. The six realms of samsara are all filled with suffering. Therefore, one should not wish to be reborn into the cycle of samsara, as it is a realm of complete suffering.

Does anything in samsara truly make sense? Possessing material wealth, power, attendants, or even loving relatives and friends will ultimately mean nothing at the time of death. The only way forward is to renounce samsara immediately and attain liberation. Let go of the ways of the conditional world. Release the notion that happiness is always positive and sorrow is always negative. Renounce these two polarizing concepts. Dualistic ideas that divide the mind are what give rise to the cycle of samsara. We must free ourselves from the dualistic concepts that only agitate the natural state of the mind. Practice the Dharma and strive to remain at ease in a state of equanimity.

Your progress truly depends on correctly understanding these four points. There is no time to be misled by the deceptive ego. There is no time for reckless laughter, silly jokes, or frivolous conversation. If you cannot sincerely engage with these four points that turn the mind toward Dharma, you will struggle to progress on the path and awaken to your true self-nature.

While reciting these four points, you must sincerely pray and take them to heart. After reciting them, take some time to contemplate their meaning. Integrate these four points into your daily life and apply them consistently in your practice. Do not part from these four points when working in the office, meeting with your friends, or being intimate with your partner. Upon waking in the morning, think of these four points. When walking, lying down, or sleeping, keep them in your heart. Make these four points your close companions in all that you do in your daily life.

These four points are like a spur that encourages you to remain on the path and adhere to the Dharma. If these four points are not addressed, the Dharma books you read, the Gurus you meet, and the empowerments you receive will mean nothing. You must examine yourself constantly! Are you inseparable from these four points? If you are a genuine practitioner, you will never be separated from these four points. Then, when it comes to practicing Dzogchen, there will be no barriers. By living with these four points, you create the karma to understand deeply. May you meditate on these four points, and may all spiritual seekers turn their minds to Dharma!

WAY OF THE BODHISATTVA

Practicing the bodhisattva path involves the six *paramitas* of transcendent wisdom and compassion. The six *paramitas* are: generosity, discipline, patience, diligence, meditation, and wisdom. Bodhisattvas conduct their lives by practicing these six *paramitas*.

It is truly profound to live as a compassionate bodhisattva, which is to live unselfishly. Consequently, bodhisattvas can assume various forms according to the needs of sentient beings. It is said that the bodhisattva's courage and confidence are such that they can manifest in whatever form is necessary to help liberate sentient beings from suffering. Additionally, it is challenging to imagine the vast number of bodhisattvas; there could be as many as the grains of sand on a beach.

You can become a true bodhisattva for your spouse, children, friends, neighbors, and even your enemies. There are countless ways in which sentient beings are in need. It is so beautiful to witness this flexibility—open to any possibility or circumstance. This willingness to engage deeply and connect with the essence of every being without judgment or condemnation is truly inspiring.

The most profound practice of the bodhisattva is the generosity of sharing wisdom teachings, which helps others to understand the true purpose of their precious human lives. Nothing is more generous than offering the teachings of Dharma, and those who engage in this activity are true bodhisattvas. The bodhisattva acts only for the benefit of all sentient beings; they harbor no personal agendas.

Bodhisattvas persevere even when their teachings are misunderstood. This reflects the bodhisattva's morality, demonstrating a commitment to continue indefinitely without fatigue. Their wisdom is vast and fluid, transcending discrimination.

The bodhisattva's practice of the *paramita* of generosity protects from danger and harm. When people experience fear and insecurity, the bodhisattva instills strength and fosters trust in their inherent abilities. Bodhisattvas are not narrow-minded and do not judge or belittle others. Their compassion is all-pervasive, shining brightly like the rays of the sun.

For the bodhisattva, the *paramita* of ethical discipline entails recognizing that selfishness is morally wrong. Any hint of selfishness can compromise the bodhisattva's ethical discipline.

The *paramita* of patience involves the capacity to forbear. When we react impulsively, we fail to exercise this endurance and miss the chance to observe the gap between the action and our response. Recognizing this space is essential. Achieving this clarity, we find no reason to react negatively. Without patience, we justify our stance and stay stuck in conditioned thinking.

The *paramita* of diligence is practiced with joyful effort and constant vigilance.

The *paramita* of meditation is guarding and maintaining awareness in the continuum of nowness.

The *paramita* of wisdom is insight, recognizing the essence of mind, which is clear and unconditional knowing. Bodhisattvas dedicate their lives to helping those who have not yet realized the essence of being. The true nature of mind embodies perfect wisdom. While study, logic, and contemplation are essential tools, we must not cling to them as ultimate truth; they are merely pointers along the way. We must realize the wisdom that goes beyond clinging to concepts.

When we arise from our meditation, we are willing to roll up our sleeves and go to work for the sake of all sentient beings. In meditation, we dwell in our essence and maintain awareness of nowness. When involved in action, in real life, so to speak, life transforms into the action of compassionate practice. For instance, when drinking a glass of water, we drink for the sake of all beings. When we quench our thirst, we rejoice, as our wish to quench the thirst of all sentient beings is achieved. Everything we do is for the sake of all sentient beings. Everyone becomes our friend, helping us to progress on the path to complete enlightenment.

The bodhisattva's wisdom is profound and extensive, like the vast ocean. Discursive thoughts and unsettling emotions resemble the waves on the ocean's surface. Bodhisattvas remain undisturbed by the tumult of the waves because they reside in the serene vastness of the sea.

Bodhisattvas champion the awakened state, the intuitive expression of enlightened intelligence. They have confidence in the mind's clear nature and are always willing to apply their intelligence to guide others. The bodhisattva has a golden heart and excludes no one. When offering a feast of Dharma to sentient beings, the bodhisattva welcomes everyone to the table.

I suggest you all take the bodhisattva vow when you feel ready to serve all of humanity. Nothing will bring you greater joy than benefiting others, and nothing will hurt you more than harming them. This is the noble way to grow and mature spiritually in this life. Bodhisattvas act for the benefit of all sentient beings and do not abandon anyone. They understand that all phenomena are empty of inherent existence; therefore, bodhisattvas are resilient, knowing that everything is workable.

Bodhisattvas engage with all thoughts and feelings, purifying them at their source with stainless awareness. Bodhisattvas are likened to warriors because they remain tireless, vigilant, and undeterred. As a Dharma practitioner, it is your responsibility to embody the qualities of a bodhisattva until you attain complete awakening; you can't delegate this responsibility to anyone else. The bodhisattva's compassion is such that they cannot turn away from suffering beings. For the bodhisattva, two arms are not enough; they emulate the bodhisattva Avalokiteshvara with one thousand arms.

•••

Question: If an individual does not want a bodhisattva's help, does the bodhisattva move on to someone else?

Rinpoche: The bodhisattva is always willing to work for others' benefit, even when they are not ready to open up. The bodhisattva sees that sentient beings suffer from the afflictions of desire, anger, ignorance, envy, and pride, and provides the essential medicine that cures the disease of samsara.

Bodhisattvas never abandon anyone. No matter how badly people behave, they recognize there is always potential for change. Bodhisattvas never fall into the sleep of ignorance; their eyes stay "wide open" day and night, full of compassion for suffering beings.

Question: When you take the bodhisattva vow, is the vow your commitment to become a bodhisattva?

Rinpoche: Yes, you do not see any alternative because any other path would be a compromise. You can't afford to compromise, as you hold yourself to such a high standard. Then, the bodhisattva's way is a win-win for oneself and others!

UNCONDITIONAL INTELLIGENCE

Good morning, everyone. It's a beautiful day with sunshine, a clear sky, and lush green trees. Here, *samaya*-bound, like-minded people gather in this sacred space to enjoy and appreciate living fully. This is the true path of meaningful Dharma.

Furthermore, as we appreciate these moments, we recognize that this day is transient. This lovely weather and our time together will not last for long. We learn to appreciate what we have here. But we do not attach to this mirage-like experience that is like a dream. Nothing we experience here is lasting or worthy of holding onto. Therefore, the most intelligent way is to remain completely unconditioned by whatever we experience in the moment.

Ordinarily, most of the time we fall into extremes. Prince Siddhartha went into the forest to find a balanced way of living and discovered the middle way. The middle way is to be free from extremes, such as nihilism and eternalism. Believing that things that we see and feel are inherently real is an extreme belief.

Enlightened beings are free from all extremes. Great meditators relate to things in a balanced way. We take refuge in the nectar-like teachings of the Awakened One and follow in his footsteps. Shakyamuni Buddha showed us the path and directed us to our true essence. When taking refuge in your unconditional nature, you advance swiftly on the spiritual path.

The Buddhist path frees us from conditional ways of thinking. Your greatest friend is your unconditional intelligence, which is never affected by the limiting concepts of past, present, and future, and is never confused by habitual patterns. This non-conceptual intelligence is beyond words and intellect. You experience it, but there's no way to fully express it. We all have the right to live freely in this liberated state of well-being and ease. This is our birthright, and nothing is more fulfilling. Practices like meditation, mantra recitation, and prayer are skillful means that help reveal the absolute state of complete freedom.

•••

Question: How can I live without being conditioned.

Rinpoche: If "you" think you are listening to "me," you are already conditioning. There is a solid me over here and a solid you over there that appear to be separate. This is conditioning. The "Jane" that you believe to be yourself and the "Rinpoche" that you see over here create the confusion of dualistic conditioning. Then, "you" and "I" seem to have distinct identities.

When there is duality, there is conditioning. For example, when "Jane" is chanting mantras, and there is the sound of "mantras" being recited, both are actually just echoes. In the echoes, there is no identifiable possessor. When you understand that, you recite mantras unconditionally, without the illusion of a separate subject and object.

Question: What is compassion?

Rinpoche: Compassion is the liberated experience of unconditional being. Compassion is intelligence. Compassion is being kind, caring, and sensitive. When you see the preciousness of human life, you feel compassion for all beings. When you are selfish, there is little compassion.

Question: As I grow older, I want to do less and less. Could this be a positive thing?

Rinpoche: When practicing Dharma, you dwell inside and look within. You may be doing less, but this could be positive, so long as you don't become distracted and spend all your time lazily playing poker, watching TV, or searching for a friend on the web.

Old age, sickness, and death are not to be feared. They are reminders to seize the moment and free ourselves from confusion and conditional limitations. We find our strength in unconditional intelligence and never place our trust in what is exhaustible, temporary, and impermanent.

PURE ASPIRATION

The teachings of the Buddha guide us on the path to awakening. We listen to the Dharma, reflect on the teachings, and meditate to embark on this path. We strive to liberate ourselves and others from the three kinds of suffering that characterize cyclic existence. We dedicate ourselves to practice with sincere motivation to benefit all sentient beings.

When interacting with others, stay mindful and alert. Reflect on your intentions. Are you pursuing personal gain? Are you protecting your ego? Are you hoping for praise or recognition? If there are strings attached, you will always anticipate something in return. In subtle ways, you'll only reinforce a self-centered mindset.

With genuine aspiration, you practice generosity. One form of generosity involves relinquishing attachment to your physical body or your ingrained beliefs. When you strongly identify with your material form or your intellect, you overlook the sacredness of being. Flesh, blood, and bone are impermanent and lack essential essence. In contrast, your true nature is unchanging, eternally pure luminous awareness.

An angry and aggressive person is tormented by uncontrollable thoughts. A fleeting thought that triggers anger can be likened to an illusion, similar to a mirage. An angry thought has no true root or foundation; it is a creation of a confused mind, and the person suffering from anger endures unnecessary pain.

With a genuine desire to be helpful, you cultivate compassion and a heartfelt wish to alleviate the suffering of others. When you follow the path of Buddha, you aspire to open yourself to all beings and, therefore, do not impose a specific point of view. You accept everyone as they are, and this dynamic power is transformative. You express yourself honestly, without bias or partiality.

Dedicate the merit you have gathered through your practice to all beings. Your practice is misguided if you fail to dedicate your merit and hoard it only for yourself. When you dedicate your merit, you honor the preciousness of life itself, and express your compassion for all sentient beings.

After dedicating your merit, you return to the world with humility, free from arrogance and pride. You embrace your genuineness, confident that all things are manageable. You demonstrate that you are a worthy being, living your life meaningfully and with purpose. Both you and the world will benefit, and everyone will find reason to celebrate.

ON RINPOCHE'S BIRTHDAY

The day of our birth is the first sign that there will be change, there will be decay, and ultimately, there will be so-called death. Therefore, a birthday could remind us of our impending demise. From the day of our birth, we never grow younger. So, our birthday is a special day to remember the transience of life. Nothing conditional lasts forever. The way to celebrate is to treasure, right now, this very moment.

So today is my birthday, I suppose. In our society, we celebrate birthdays. When we are young, we enjoy birthdays and never think about death. As we age, we often forget about our birthdays because we don't want to think about getting old and cannot accept it. The way to face inevitable change is to go deep within yourself to reveal the unconditional nature of your being, which is beyond death, destruction, and change.

You may agree that change is taking place and that conditional things are transient, but if you fixate on that understanding as just a thought in your head, that is a mere conceptual understanding. To truly understand, you have to experience the reality of death and impermanence. That is to say, you need to be uncompromising and fearless in your approach to life.

Usually, we resist and try to ignore the truth. The problem is we *think* we exist as a solid entity; we *think* that we die, and our thoughts seem to make it very real. We have to recognize that thoughts are not the experience, and the experience is not the thoughts. Thoughts are deceiving; direct experience is clear and undeniable. This is the wonder of freedom beyond living and dying, beyond a beginning and end.

A birthday is a day to have more clarity and insight into the value of relating to all things unconditionally. Here, there is a sense of stability, where one does not fall into extremes, such as good versus bad or right versus wrong. When conditioned by our beliefs and habits, there is no equilibrium, no balance.

We create our own suffering by pursuing unrealistic expectations, which stem from ignorance—we fail to recognize that all conditioned things are impermanent and subject to change. You can embrace impermanence and change when you stop trying to hold on to a moment that is always vanishing.

You can also celebrate by reflecting on the Buddha's life and qualities, including his unselfish sharing of wisdom and compassion, his freedom from attachment to worldly concerns, and his liberation of others from suffering. Read the life stories of the Buddha and other great masters and try to emulate how they lived and achieved awakening for themselves and others. Aspire to follow in their footsteps.

These are meaningful ways to celebrate your birthday. Furthermore, every day is an appropriate time to reflect on impermanence and death. We are born, and we die every second. We may feel we are the same old person living the same old life. But our life is like a river, constantly flowing, never the same. Every moment is a fresh new river. Life is like that—each moment your life is born in a fresh new moment—a fresh new life! Birth and death happen at every moment. So, we have reason to celebrate when we remain in the continuum of awareness. This is clarity, and this is wisdom!

We all wish to enjoy every moment fully without hesitation, but we often hold back; we retreat. Clinging to our ego, we feel insecure. We fear losing ourselves because we mistakenly perceive the ego as our true identity and try to protect it. We withdraw into a world of false stability, shielding ourselves from the truth of impermanence and change. If birth and death occur in every moment, what is there left to defend? Who is truly there to protect? It would be your good fortune to find the courage to embrace perfect freedom in each moment.

The way to face change is to loosen the knots of habitual grasping. Then, you begin to see things more clearly. As you see things clearly, there is no reason to be afraid. You recognize that fear is a result of your grasping for a solid self-identity. When you are crippled by fear, you cannot see clearly. You limit yourself, and you suffer the consequences. We generally feel that something outside is the cause of our torment, but the suffering comes from the inside out. Ultimately, all suffering is of our own making.

When faced with a challenge, strive to see clearly and avoid being affected by fleeting situations and circumstances. Remember the perfect moment—the moment that is free, unbounded, and unconditioned. Reawaken to your unconditional wisdom nature. This is the wisdom that does not cling to a rigid or contrived sense of "me."

I like to celebrate my birthday by reawakening this precious freedom. This is not possible when you perpetuate your habitual views. The extremes of liking and disliking come from trying to pick and choose the conditions that suit you. Then, you are controlled by ego's habits. You can celebrate when you are free of conditioning. You dance in that moment. As you dance, you lose the sense of yourself as the dancer. This is the celebration of free, unconditioned energy; this is valuing and appreciating your life.

We limit ourselves. We do not recognize that we have constructed a self-identity that does not truly exist. This is what I call "burdened by extra baggage." When letting go of the baggage, we experience freedom. We can examine ourselves to see how much extra baggage we have accumulated. When you are a newborn, you don't carry extra baggage. The older we get, the more and more baggage we carry.

Imagine a young child with a new toy truck. They are thrilled as they drive it on the floor, the table, and even the walls. They are fully absorbed. Soon after, they've forgotten about it and are experiencing something new and fresh. To celebrate your birthday, become like a child again—innocent, fearless, and unaffected—completely present in the moment. I invite everyone to join me in being innocent and childlike on my birthday! (*Rinpoche and students laugh together.*)

JUST A SHORT STAY

This life of ours is like a brief stay at an inn. We pay for a cozy little room, which is our good fortune. Maybe we can even afford a suite at a five-star hotel. Either way, we have a comfortable shelter, and in this sense, we are fortunate.

Wouldn't it be wise to relax and enjoy a peaceful stay? However, as soon as we settle in, we notice faults in our room. There is a crack in the wall, so we go out and buy some plaster. But once the wall is patched, we realize the color doesn't match, so we return to the store for some paint and spend some time painting the wall. Later, we notice the room's decor is not to our liking, so we move the rug and rearrange the furniture. Tired from all our exertion, we lie down for a nap, but the mattress is lumpy, so we head to the store to buy a new one. When we return, we discover that the toilet in the bathroom is leaking. By the time we fix the plumbing, the sun will be setting, and our stay will be over.

Now it's time to check out. Unfortunately, we were unable to relax, and we left the hotel feeling worn out and grouchy. This is how we misuse our lives, forgetting that our time here is short and fleeting. How much time should we invest in worldly affairs and material possessions? How much should we obsess over conditions that are unstable, ephemeral, and constantly changing?

You need to reach a turning point where you become more practical and resolute. During this brief journey we call life, don't fuss too much about flaws and imperfections. All conditions are uncertain. Whatever happens in the moment is just so. If your car breaks down on the highway, respond appropriately and don't waste time complaining. If your boss is throwing a tantrum and swearing at you, it's okay because, after all, bosses do get angry. If there's nothing you can do to change or defuse his anger, why get upset? With mindfulness, you will be able to handle circumstances gracefully. Let's not waste our precious breath trying to change what already is. Invest your time in what brings enduring fulfillment and satisfaction. This is the best way to spend your short stay!

Guru Padmasambhava

PART TWO
DZOGCHEN TEACHINGS

THE PRAYER OF CALLING THE LAMA FROM AFAR

by His Holiness Dudjom Rinpoche
with commentary by His Eminence Shyalpa Tenzin Rinpoche

The essence, primordially unchanging, the innate nature,
free from elaboration,
Dwells as the youthful vase body, the originally pure,
profound clarity.
Dharmakaya Lama, Yeshe Dorje, you who know,
Please grant the blessings to attain great confidence in the view.

The nature, unceasing, conjoined configuration of luminous
clarity,
Dwells as the display of the spontaneously present five
certainties.
Sambhogakaya Lama, Dechen Dorje, you who know,
Please grant blessings to perfect great ability in meditation.

Compassion, without bias, primordial wisdom free from
all limitations,
Dwells as the essence of all-pervading naked
awareness-emptiness.
Nirmanakaya Lama, Drodul Lingpa, you who know,
Please grant the blessings to accomplish great progress in action.

The primordial ground of one's awareness is unchanging and
unmoving.
Whatever arises as the expression of the dharmakaya is neither
good nor bad.
Since awareness of nowness is the actual buddha,
The completely free, serene Lama is revealed in one's
innermost heart.

When this original mind is realized as the very nature of
the Lama,
There is no need for whining or contrived prayers made with
grasping and attachment.
By letting go, in the free flow of uncontrived awareness,
Not holding onto whatever arises, the blessing of self-liberation
is obtained.

With fabricated practice, there is no chance to achieve
enlightenment.
This meditation, produced through mental analysis and intellect
is a deceiving enemy.
Now, conceptualization falls apart with the abandon of
a madman.
Let this life be spent in a state of uninhibited, naked ease!

Whatever one does is joyful, practitioner of Dzogchen,
the Great Perfection!
In any company, happy, lineage heir of the Lotus-Born!
Protector without rival, great treasure-revealing Lama!
Teachings beyond compare; heart essence of the dakinis!

Having dispelled the heart's darkness, great ignorance,
in its own place,
The undiminished sun of luminous clarity shines continuously.

This good fortune is the kindness of the Lama, the only father.
Unrepayable kindness! Only remember the Lama!

The Commentary

Verse 1

The essence, primordially unchanging, the innate nature,
free from elaboration,
Dwells as the youthful vase body, the originally pure,
profound clarity.

His Holiness Dudjom Rinpoche says the essence of mind is primordially unchanging and free from conceptual elaboration.

According to the Dzogchen tradition, the "youthful vase body" dwells within all beings. This youthful vase body is unconditional, luminous wisdom beyond birth, old age, decay, and death; hence, it is described as youthful. It is spontaneously accomplished insight, a sacred body of unobstructed primordial wisdom that is innately clear. This subtle wisdom usually goes unrecognized, like a candle burning in a vase. The youthful vase body is the enlightened kayas: dharmakaya, sambhogakaya, and nirmanakaya.

The unconditional body is the pure, luminous space in which the "I" as such does not inherently exist. When recognizing that the "I" does not exist, the conditional sense of "I" is shattered.

In Dzogchen, it is shown that the primordially pure nature is perfect from the very beginning. Therefore, the practice is to realize this view and become inseparable from this pure, profound clarity.

Dharmakaya Lama, Yeshe Dorje, you who know,
Please grant blessings to attain great confidence in the view.

Here, you pray to the dharmakaya Lama—the absolute nature of mind itself—to have confidence in this most profound view of the indestructible wisdom of Dzogchen, so that conceptual thoughts are liberated within the natural flow of unobstructed energy. You will gain confidence in this view by knowing that the essence of your being is primordially pure and perfect.

You might wonder, where is this essence? Is it in my heart, my head, my mind? Here, it shouldn't be complicated. When a thought arises, there appears to be the so-called "I" who experiences the thought.

Ordinarily, you feel that I am just myself, and this "I" seems very real and concrete. But this "I" is just a label, created by discursive thoughts, which obscure your natural freshness and independence. When you believe in this "I," you are not seeing this fundamentally pure nature that goes beyond conceptualization. This "I" is the result of ignorance and habitual thoughts. There is this seemingly imperfect "I" that you have created, but it is not your true nature.

Thoughts are the creative display of the mind's dynamic energy. When one fails to recognize the mind's true nature, thoughts lead to dualistic conceptions and an endless cycle of conflict, leaving one feeling weak and restless. Ignorance of one's true nature is like a thief that robs one of awareness of nowness. Recognizing the true nature of thoughts brings great confidence in the view —the fundamental space free of root or basis.

Your meditation will mean little if you do not understand this crucial point: there is no "I" you can identify as truly existent, no concrete "I" as such to cling to. Do not continually entangle yourself in a web of thoughts. When you do, the very fresh moment of awareness is lost. Solidifying the thoughts and the thinker as inherently real is the cause of all suffering.

Verse 2

The nature, unceasing, conjoined configuration of luminous clarity,
Dwells as the display of the spontaneously present five certainties.

The luminous clarity is the configuration of the five certainties: the certainty of the teacher, the certainty of the teachings, the certainty of the place, the certainty of disciples, and the certainty of the time. The teacher is luminous awareness. The teachings are the inexpressible truth beyond words. The place is the mandala of blissful awareness. The disciples reflect the continuum of self-awareness. The time is this very moment beyond past, present, and future.

Sambhogakaya Lama, Dechen Dorje, you who know,
Please grant the blessings to perfect great ability in meditation.

Here, you invoke the blessings of the Lama so you can perfect your ability in meditation. In meditation, luminous clarity is the expression of pure, unobstructed energy. Here, you realize that nothing meaningful can be achieved by doing. You familiarize yourself with this luminously clear state, like the sun shining brightly in a cloudless sky. This meditative state of samadhi is carefree and complete.

Verse 3

Compassion, without bias, primordial wisdom free from all limitations,
Dwells as the essence of all-pervading naked awareness-emptiness.

Compassion is the dynamic force of wisdom that is unbiased and free of agenda. It is free from all extremes, free of concepts, and free from attachment. It is all-pervading awareness-emptiness, naked and fresh. This awareness is not conditioned by concepts of this and that. It is free of all limiting constructs.

Nirmanakaya Lama, Drodul Lingpa, you who know,
Please grant the blessings to accomplish great progress in action.

This is the nirmanakaya Lama. Nirmanakaya represents the manifestation of the compassionate expression of enlightenment. Yeshe Dorje means indestructible wisdom. Dechen Dorje means indestructible great bliss. And Drodul Lingpa means "one who tames beings and subjugates ego." These three names represent the three kayas, the inseparable characteristics of the enlightened wisdom mind.

The precious Lama is the embodiment of Buddha, Dharma, and Sangha; the embodiment of Guru, yidam, and dakini; the embodiment of dharmakaya, sambhogakaya, and nirmanakaya; and the embodiment of the essence, nature, and compassionate expression of the three kayas.

The Prayer of Calling the Lama From Afar was composed by the revered master His Holiness Dudjom Rinpoche, Jigdral Yeshe Dorje. I received this teaching from my root teacher, Kyabje Chatral Sangye Dorje Rinpoche, who received it from Dudjom Rinpoche. Here, we do not see the Lama as merely a physical body of flesh and blood; instead, we recognize the true wisdom Lama—the natural essence of our own mind. Yeshe Dorje, Dechen Dorje, and Drodul Lingpa are three Tibetan names for Dudjom Rinpoche that correspond to view, meditation, and action, respectively.

In the tradition of Great Perfection, you approach the Lama with devotion, trust, and respect, and the Lama invokes the unconditional wisdom that dwells within you.

Verse 4

The primordial ground of one's awareness is unchanging and unmoving.
Whatever arises as the expression of the dharmakaya is neither good nor bad.

The primordial nature, pristine awareness, is free from transformation and change. This pure nature can neither be defiled nor sanctified. Believing that we are becoming better or worse is merely a fabrication of conceptual thought, which has no validity. Ultimately, all that appears in the mind is the display of dharmakaya, the essence of mind. The practice here is to realize that whatever arises in the mind is the display of emptiness inseparable from appearances.

Since awareness of nowness is the actual buddha,
The completely free, serene Lama is revealed in one's innermost heart.

The actual buddha is awareness of nowness, which is free of the times of past, present, and future. Concepts of time are conditional; awareness of nowness is timeless. Time is constructed using concepts, while awareness of nowness is the awakened buddha within all beings.

One's innermost heart is recognized as the completely free, serene Lama, the beginningless ground of awakened awareness that never changes or transforms into something else.

Verse 5

When this original mind is realized as the very nature of the Lama,
There is no need for whining or contrived prayers made with grasping and attachment.

When your original mind is revealed, everything becomes a prayer for you. You don't need a special prayer to maintain your awareness. Resting in the unwavering state of pure awareness becomes your prayer. The song of a bird singing in the forest is your prayer to the Lama. The patter of rain on your roof is a prayer to emptiness. The brilliant light of the summer sun is a prayer to awakening.

But of course, until one reaches this state of unwavering awareness, one may need to recite contrived prayers because one relies on the kind Lama for guidance and encouragement.

By letting go, in the free flow of uncontrived awareness,
Not holding onto whatever arises, the blessing of self-liberation is obtained.

Remain in this natural continuum of uncontrived awareness. You do not cling to good or bad. Your thoughts cannot distract you. Without grasping or attachment, all appearances are self-liberated. Whatever appears, don't fixate. Don't try to put it in a box. As soon as you do, it becomes conditioned. Then, where is the joy? Where is the freedom?

Let each thought self-liberate and rest in the natural state of your being.

Verse 6

With fabricated practice, there is no chance to achieve enlightenment.
This meditation, produced through mental analysis and intellect is a deceiving enemy.

Fabricated practice is unnatural. When you conceptualize with the intellect, you are not in the natural state of dharmakaya. If you think your meditation is getting worse, you try to fix it. If you think your meditation is getting better, you feel good. If you are unaware that all thoughts arise and vanish in space-like emptiness, you will be fooled by your discursive thoughts.

Now, conceptualization falls apart with the abandon of a madman.
Let this life be spent in a state of uninhibited, naked ease!

Aah! How freeing this is, to be naturally at ease! The ego always needs to protect and defend itself. This is inhibiting. The ego is confined, caught between "should" and "should not." Living in a natural state of uninhibited naked ease, a practitioner of the Great Perfection is not constrained by the egocentric self.

Verse 7

Whatever one does is joyful, practitioner of Dzogchen, the Great Perfection!
In any company, happy, lineage heir of the Lotus-Born!

Those who are blessed by the lineage, blessed by transmission and empowerment, recognize that all appearances are expressions of dharmakaya. There is freedom and therefore, everything is joyful. The practitioner of the Great Perfection sees everything as a natural expression of emptiness.

There is no place, circumstance, or thought that is not joyful. If you go to hell, that is acceptable. If you go to heaven, that is acceptable. Any company, any circumstance, any situation, any idea, is workable. You inherit the lineage of the Lotus-Born, the great master, Padmasambhava. You are happy and carefree because all things self-liberate into emptiness.

You might believe you understand the view of Great Perfection, but if you find yourself caught up in mental afflictions and disruptive emotions, you still have more work to do on the spiritual journey. You may think you know Dzogchen, but you haven't experienced it directly. You are not yet a true lineage holder of pure awareness.

Protector without rival, great treasure-revealing Lama!
Teachings beyond compare; heart essence of the dakinis!

The Lama reveals to you the treasury of the Great Perfection and protects you from going astray and falling into an abyss. This treasure-revealing Lama, with teachings beyond compare, is without rival!

Verse 8

Having dispelled the heart's darkness, great ignorance, in its own place,
The undiminished sun of luminous clarity shines continuously.

When the sun of luminous clarity shines, ignorance dissolves in its own place. "Its own place" is the vast space of emptiness. In the moment of luminous clarity, there is no darkness. This luminosity shines continuously, without beginning or end.

This good fortune is the kindness of the Lama, the only father. Unrepayable kindness! Only remember the Lama!

This good fortune is the kindness of the Lama, who embodies the unconditional love that is within you. This wisdom Lama is the ultimate unconditional refuge. You can never repay the Lama's kindness. To only remember the Lama is to remember that all phenomenal appearances are expressions of luminous emptiness. Remain continually in awareness of nowness with heartfelt conviction.

•••

Question: Is it correct that one should not try to stop thoughts?

Rinpoche: There is no sense in trying to stop your thoughts. Understand that thoughts are merely manifesting from the energetic display of awareness. Thoughts will come, but they will self-liberate if you recognize the root of all thoughts, which is ignorance. Do not chase after thoughts or cling to them; leave them be. Then, you are free from grasping at thoughts. You are not trapped or controlled by thoughts, and this is perfect freedom.

Question: In the practice of meditation, should one be a witness of thoughts?

Rinpoche: That would be a practice for beginners only. Thoughts are the energy display of dharmakaya, which is emptiness. The essence of the thought is empty of any solid ground or root. The practice in Dzogchen is to see the actual nature of thoughts as they arise.

Here, this practice is not to witness the thoughts. You see how every thought dissolves into the space of dharmakaya, like a wave receding into the ocean. The point is that witnessing the thoughts is just the first step. The key is to realize that thoughts have no intrinsic existence.

Question: When you see that your thoughts have no intrinsic existence, would that threaten your sense of identity? Your ego might not like that?

Rinpoche: Whether you like it or not, there is no choice. If your ego does not like it, you can laugh at the ego and say, "You may not like it, but you have no role to play." Ego's lies are exposed. What is ego anyway? The ego is a fabrication, the creation of grasping to a contrived identity. You can do very well without ego.

This is what Calling the Lama from Afar is showing us. You will not call on the Lama to complain or cause unnecessary trouble. Your call to the Lama should bring out the best in yourself. You can email or call the Lama—that's fine. You can tell the Lama about your problems. But remembering the Lama's kindness and liberating all your thoughts on the spot is the best way to chant Calling the Lama from Afar. The Lama introduces you to the greatest of the great, your very own enlightened nature!

•••

To summarize, everything I have explained is condensed in this prayer:

Glorious root teacher, precious one,
Dwelling on the lotus seat on the crown of my head,
Hold me with your great kindness,
Bestow the accomplishment of body, speech, and mind!

Glorious root teacher, precious one... You know the teacher is glorious and precious. You can have hundreds of teachers, but you only have one root teacher—the one who gives birth to your compassion and introduces you to the luminous clarity of your mind.

Dwelling on the lotus seat on the crown of my head... Out of respect and devotion, you visualize the precious teacher on the crown of your head.

Hold me with your great kindness... You invoke the kind teacher and pray that the teacher looks after you because you want to accomplish what is meaningful and purposeful in your life.

Bestow the accomplishment of body, speech, and mind! You ask the teacher to bestow upon you sacred body, speech, and mind. You vow not to dwell in mundane body, speech, and mind. You promise to remain inseparable from your kind root teacher, now and forever.

Lama, please think of me!
Lama, please think of me!
Lama, please think of me!

Lama khyenno!
Lama khyenno!
Lama khyenno!

DEVOTION IN THE LINEAGE OF PADMASAMBHAVA

We begin every practice with the pure motivation to benefit all sentient beings. Every practice is done for the benefit of all. Our overall practice depends upon understanding the four points that turn the mind toward Dharma. The more deeply one understands the significance of these four points, the more motivated and determined one will be to practice the pure Dharma.

In practicing Dharma, there are many traditions one can follow within the three vehicles of hinayana, mahayana, and vajrayana. These teachings depend on one's interest and capacity. Whichever vehicle suits you is the one you should practice, without thinking that one view is lower or higher than another. Although vajrayana is the most profound in its view and practice, that does not mean it is always the best choice for everyone.

On the vajrayana path, you have devotion when you understand and appreciate the profundity of the teachings and the lineage. The Guru's great kindness, wisdom, and compassion for all sentient beings characterize the vajrayana path. The Guru embodies the wisdom and compassion of all enlightened beings, the realization of emptiness and awareness—the nature of mind itself. The Guru sees that beings suffer due to ignorance of the mind's true nature. A Guru who has realized the wisdom of emptiness shows us the path to freedom from suffering. The Guru's compassionate activity is unceasing, like the sun shining brightly without beginning or end. The activities of the Guru are boundless, like the sky.

The Buddha foretold that Padmasambhava would appear in this dark age with swift and effective methods to liberate beings from suffering. There is nothing more profound than the teachings and practices of Guru Padmasambhava. Padmasambhava and his enlightened consort, Yeshe Tsogyal, planted the seeds of vajrayana across the land of Tibet, and these precious teachings have been preserved and are still available to us today. Furthermore, it is said that if you pray to Guru Padmasambhava with sincere trust and devotion, he will appear before you and guide you in your practice.

The extraordinary lineage of Guru Padmasambhava has been transmitted from teacher to disciple for over 1,400 years. Over the centuries, this golden lineage was passed on from Padmasambhava to such luminaries as Longchenpa, Jigme Lingpa, and countless other great lineage masters, such as Patrul Rinpoche and Khenpo Ngawang Pelzang, and on to my glorious, incomparable kind root teacher, Chatral Rinpoche, Sangye Dorje.

These most profound teachings are not always readily available to the public and are often given in private, according to each individual's capacity and level of understanding. In Dzogchen, devotion and faith in the Lama are indispensable. When the student is ready, the Lama introduces the student to the nature of mind itself. So, trust between the teacher and the student is essential. If the student is sincere and genuine, the teacher responds in kind.

The relationship between Milarepa and his teacher, Marpa, exemplifies mutual trust and respect. At the first meeting with Marpa, Milarepa felt great faith and devotion and requested teachings from Marpa. However, Marpa did not offer any teachings to Milarepa; instead, he put him to work. Marpa accepted Milarepa as his student, and Milarepa demonstrated his devotion and commitment to Dharma, surrendering to Marpa's commands. The inexpressible essence of the Buddha's teaching was transmitted in this way.

Practitioners begin by first meditating on the preciousness of human life and on death and impermanence. For instance, meditation on death refers to the dissolution of the physical body composed of material elements. The material body dies; however, the primordially pure mind is deathless. Padmasambhava realized the undying essence of timeless awareness. Therefore, when praying to Padmasambhava, the Guru will appear to those with faith and devotion.

In Dzogchen, one realizes space-like emptiness—the luminous nature of the mind—which is boundless like the sky. One sees how the concept of impermanence is empty by nature; it is merely a fleeting thought. Death as such is also a thought. Beyond words and labels, there is neither birth nor death. Essentially, there is no "self" that dies.

In the clear light of pure awareness, all thoughts are exhausted. There is only the unobstructed display of the energy of primordial wisdom beyond the conditioned mind. Guru Padmasambhava displayed the rainbow body of great transference, dissolving into a celestial realm. This is why, for devoted practitioners, Padmasambhava's blessings can be so powerful for spiritual seekers.

There are many levels of understanding of the Buddha's teachings, as presented in hinayana, mahayana, vajrayana, and Dzogchen, so you cannot just assume that you have reached the depth and pinnacle of the Buddha's teachings. For example, in the hinayana and mahayana, there is no discussion of *kadak*, primordial purity, or *lhundrup*, spontaneous accomplishment. In the definitive teachings of Dzog chen, the realization of deathlessness is the one medicine that cures all disease. It is the perfect cure for impermanence, for old age, sickness, and death.

In Dzogchen, it's important to trust in the Lama's compassion and kindness. If the Lama criticizes you, don't automatically assume that the Lama is being unkind. It might be a valuable lesson for you. It all depends on your level of commitment and your ability to surrender your ego. The outcome is entirely up to you.

Nevertheless, wherever there is ego, there is suffering. However, we all wish to be free from suffering. Generate compassion for yourself and all beings, and understand that the ego is merely the result of ignorance, that is, not knowing your true nature.

•••

Question: How can we strengthen our faith and devotion?

Rinpoche: Try to see the Guru as an emanation of Padmasambhava. Sit before a picture of your Guru. Imagine the Guru is actually there in front of you. Visualize your Guru or Padmasambhava as a body of light. Feel grateful for the Guru's unconditional kindness. Feel the depth of your devotion and respect. Surrender your ordinary, conditioned mind and receive the radiance of the Guru's powerful blessings.

When distracted, you can waste your precious time. You might accomplish many worldly things, but these would be only ordinary accomplishments, not the great accomplishment of realizing your true nature. The great accomplishment is taming your unruly mind and liberating desire, aggression, and delusion. Even washing a glass in the sink or preparing your meal could be great accomplishment. If you can do these mundane tasks with pure, undistracted awareness, then that is great accomplishment itself!

The Lineage of *Pema Sangtig*

PRAYER TO THE GURU

from the Pema Sangtig Ngondro

Before practicing the ngondro, generate pure motivation. When awakening in the morning, instead of rushing to the kitchen for a cup of coffee, sit up on your bed for a few minutes and promise yourself that whatever you do today will be not only for your benefit but for the benefit of all sentient beings. Make the entire day a pure expression of caring and compassion for others. In this way, your life has meaning and purpose.

Now we will practice "Prayer to the Guru," from the Pema Sangthig Ngondro, entitled *The Chariot of Omniscience, the Secret Essence of Padmasambhava*. When beginning the ngondro, we supplicate the Guru.

From the ngondro text, I will read the instructions for "Prayer to the Guru:"

For fortunate beings with virtuous karma who are receptacles for the profound path, here is the Dharma of the preliminaries, chief of activities, within which are both the general and extraordinary. First, in a secluded spot, sit on a comfortable seat, hold the key points of the body upright, clear the stale breath three times, count twenty-one times the in and out movement of the breath, and become a suitable container for samadhi.

Ah!
Above one's head, on a lotus and moon disk,
Is the root Guru, embodiment of all buddhas,
In the manner of Vajradhara,
Together with all the Vidyadhara Gurus of the three lineages,
In an expanse of dazzling five-colored lights and spheres of rainbow rays,
Sitting in the great equanimity, luminous space.

Release the impure air of desire, aversion, and ignorance, exhaling strongly three times. Then, count the in and out breaths twenty-one times.

First, visualize a lotus flower on the crown of your head. On the lotus flower is a moon disk. On the moon disk is your root Guru, sitting in deep samadhi. Appearing in the form of Vajradhara, your root teacher embodies all the buddhas of the past, present, and future. All of the lineage Gurus circle your root Guru. Your root Guru received the teachings of this profound preliminary practice from his teacher, and in this way, the lineage is passed on from teacher to disciple.

Your Guru is not an ordinary Guru by any means. Though each of us is blessed with buddha nature, one also needs the blessings of a realized lineage Guru to obtain satisfaction and confidence on the path. Your root Guru received those blessings from his teachers. That is why your Guru is surrounded by all of the Gurus of the lineage.

You should not think that all these lineage Gurus and your own Guru exist substantially as if they were made of

Vajradhara

flesh and blood. They are not. Visualize your Guru in the form of luminous Vajradhara, so your Guru is not tangible in any way. The Guru above your head could be as big or as small as you are capable of imagining.

The luminous clarity of the Guru should be clearly established; otherwise, you will have trouble integrating your practice into your daily life. Your ego will resist the physical Guru because your ego does not want to surrender to a tangible, flesh-and-blood Guru. So, first and foremost, you must recognize ego as the source of trouble. It is, therefore, essential to understand that the egocentric self is empty of inherent existence, and the Guru's form above you is luminous emptiness. When you visualize your Guru, there is nothing tangible to oppose you physically. Additionally, the luminous Guru has the power to bless you so you can attain all the physical and mental happiness you desire.

There is no ceiling above you to constrict the lineage Gurus, making them feel claustrophobic. Do not imagine the Gurus in such a narrow-minded way. To receive the Guru's blessings, visualize the mandala of the Guru and all the lineage Gurus circling everywhere in a great expanse of rainbows and spheres of five-colored light.

Your root teacher and all the lineage Gurus are in the samadhi of great equanimity. They are not black or white. They are not male or female. They are not human or non-human. They are not concept or non-concept. Do not have any dualistic ideas. Do not relate to the Gurus and lineage masters as if they were in ordinary form. These Gurus have no hope, no fear, no attachment, no desire, no anger, and no hatred whatsoever. They are all in luminous form, and their appearance is inseparable from emptiness. If you can relate to the Gurus in this way, blessings will be with you. At the supreme level, one will be able to relate to all conditioned appearances as mere displays of the luminous Guru.

Once your visualization is established, recite the prayer to the Guru many times:

I pray to the dharmakaya buddha, lord Guru,
Grant your blessing to clear away dark ignorance.
I pray to the sambogakaya Guru,
Grant your blessing for clarity to arise from within.
I pray to the compassionate nirmanakaya Guru,
Grant your blessing to accomplish the dual purpose of self and others.

First, pray to the dharmakaya buddha. Dharmakaya represents the actual state of your own mind. Your root Guru is the dharmakaya buddha, and all the blessings of the dharmakaya come to you. Pray to the dharmakaya Guru to free you from the obscurations of ignorance. All the lineage Gurus, your root Guru, and Vajradhara are inseparable from the space of emptiness. When you realize this essence, you will be free from the darkness of ignorance.

Then pray to the sambhogakaya Guru for clarity and self-realization. Clarity arises from within. Pray to the Sambhogakaya Guru that the quality of your mind will be revealed and manifest to help free you from obscurations and hindrances on the path. The quality of your mind is clarity. The quality of your mind is luminosity. The nature of your mind is free from ignorance, free from darkness. The essence of your mind is emptiness. The Guru appears or manifests from the empty essence in the form of the dharmakaya. Now, from that same empty essence, the quality of your mind manifests as the sambhogakaya Guru. That quality is clarity and luminosity.

Then you pray to the nirmanakaya Guru. The blessings of the nirmanakaya Guru can benefit you and benefit others. You help yourself by freeing yourself from the chain of ignorance and delusion. You help others by shining wisdom on those who cannot free themselves from darkness. It is like the sun. The sun shines impartially on everyone. In essence, no clouds can block the sun. Even if a dark cloud seems to be obscuring the sun, the sun itself is always shining.

When you are no longer identified with the idea of a solid, concrete "I," you realize that the "I" is empty of inherent existence. Then, clarity arises. Free from the darkness of ignorance, you can help both yourself and others.

This prayer refers to what we call *ngowo, rangzhin,* and *thugje*. In Dzogchen, *ngowo* means essence, *rangzhin* means nature, and *thugje* means energy or compassion. *Ngowo* corresponds to the dharmakaya, *rangzhin* to the sambhogakaya, and *thugje* is the nirmanakaya.

When you pray to the dharmakaya Guru, what are you asking for? You want to be free from the darkness of ignorance. When you realize that the essence of mind is emptiness, you are free from the ignorance of not knowing your true nature. When you only accumulate material things, helplessly chasing desire after desire, you should pause and ask yourself, "Why am I doing this?" You are caught chasing after material things because you are not looking into the essence of those objects; therefore, they seem concrete and solid to you. You feel that there is something to achieve, something tangible, something that truly exists. You believe that there is something separate from you that you must possess. But that is not how it truly is. Thinking in that mistaken way, there is no end to confusion and ignorance, and you will never find peace and happiness.

When you are free from darkness, what do you have? You have clarity. You have luminous wisdom. When you are free from confusion, you understand things clearly. That is wealth. That is joy. That is life. That is bliss. That is the sambhogakaya Guru. By praying to the sambhogakaya Guru, you pray that clarity may come from within. How can clarity come from within? Clarity comes from within when the Guru's wisdom mind and your mind are inseparable.

The Guru embodies all the blessings of all the buddhas of past, present, and future. Therefore, clarity and luminosity are possible, not because you imagine or believe it. It is possible to experience directly through the blessings of an unbroken stream of Gurus and lineage masters. Historically, it has been realized many times. The Guru embodies the realization of all the Gurus and lineage masters of the past, present, and future. So, you pray to the sambhogakaya Guru to receive the blessings of clarity, and through that prayer to the Guru, clarity is realized from within.

Clarity from within will benefit both yourself and others. This is the meaning of the prayer to your Guru as nirmanakaya. The benefit to self and others comes naturally from the clarity of the sambhogakaya.

This is the prayer to the dharmakaya, sambhogakaya, and nirmanakaya. If you can visualize clearly and expand your understanding to the farthest corners of the vast expanse, you will see that there is no end to the expression of these three aspects. The more you meditate, the more profound your realization and understanding.

At the Guru's forehead, OM symbolizes the body of all the buddhas and has a brilliant white color. AH at the Guru's throat symbolizes the speech of all the buddhas and is red in color. HUNG at the Guru's heart represents the mind of all the buddhas and has a dark blue color. Focus on these three centers.

Having earnestly recited the prayer over and over, focus on the Guru's three centers and begin chanting OM AH HUM. While you chant, visualize your ordinary body, speech, and mind dissolving into light and becoming inseparable from the Guru's enlightened, clear light body, speech, and mind.

(*Rinpoche chants melodiously and retreatants follow along*)

As you chant, feel the bliss and the blessings of the enlightened body, speech, and mind of the Guru, which are inseparable from you.

OM AH HUM, OM AH HUM
OM AH HUM, OM AH HUM...

See how you are truly protected from evil thoughts and all distractions. Feel the Guru's kindness and compassion. Praying with devotion to the Guru is the greatest prayer. Rest body, speech, and mind, free of all thoughts and concepts.

OM AH HUM, OM AH HUM
OM AH HUM, OM AH HUM...

The blessing of the Guru is received with a sense of great contentment and fulfillment.

Experience it. Dwell in it. Rest in it. Amazing!

OM AH HUM, OM AH HUM
OM AH HUM, OM AH HUM...

Sing OM AH HUM—a song of joy. Like a snake shedding its old skin, you are suddenly fresh. Beyond ordinary, impure mind, you are inseparable from the wisdom mind of the Guru.

OM AH HUM, OM AH HUM
OM AH HUM, OM AH HUM...

However you are, the Guru has no judgment. Whatever you think, whatever you feel is welcomed. The Guru's compassionate mind has no limit. You can chant as fast or as slow as you want. Just chant freely. No need to follow any specific rules or instructions.

OM AH HUM, OM AH HUM
OM AH HUM, OM AH HUM...

At the end of chanting, rest evenly with the Guru's mind and your mind inseparably mixed. Your realization will be at one with the Guru's. Rest here in Samadhi and remain at ease. Then complete this practice by reciting the dedication prayer:

This virtue and other virtues,
By binding all into one,
I dedicate to the space of inexhaustible dharmakaya.
May we obtain buddhahood without meeting or separating.

Always follow the three sublime practices. The first sublime practice is to generate pure altruistic intention, as I have already explained at the beginning. The second sublime practice is to invoke the Guru's unconditional blessing and to cultivate awareness of nowness without distraction. The third sublime practice is to dedicate all of the merit you have gathered for the benefit of all sentient beings and ultimately, to free yourself from dualistic mind. Without these three, your practice will not be complete.

•••

From the Sanskrit, the mantra OM AH HUM is composed of sacred sounds that energize the chakras. The syllable OM signifies enlightened body, AH signifies enlightened speech, and HUM signifies enlightened mind. Chanting OM purifies conditioned karmic actions of the body, chanting AH purifies conditioned karmic speech, and chanting HUM purifies conditioned karmic thoughts.

Spiritual life always begins with a compassionate attitude that is free of personal agendas. When we act selfishly, we condition the body, speech, and mind, and this conditioning has no lasting or ultimate benefit. When we say that samsara is repulsive, it means that all of samsara eventually fails us. We have been tricked by our selfish ways, ignoring that all compounded things are impermanent and lack true existence.

When you do the supplication prayer, visualize Vajra dhara and the Guru as luminous light. You are not surrendering to a man or woman as such; you are surrendering to the unconditional state of your being—the natural state that is primordially pure.

See the beauty in it! At first, your ego may not want to surrender, but ultimately, you have no choice. It is up to you how seriously you practice. Furthermore, remember how kind the Gurus are—they show you the way to the unconditional state of perfect freedom.

In conclusion, this mantra has great power. Recite OM AH HUM. You can practice this anywhere and recite it in any way you wish. You can even sing the mantra OM AH HUM in the shower. Through the power of the mantra, all your negativities are washed clean. You can recite it out loud, or you can whisper it to yourself. You can say it slowly or swiftly. When you finish chanting, rest naturally. Your ordinary mind and the enlightened mind of the Guru will be inseparable—like pouring water into water. If you are not doing the entire ngondro, at least do this prayer to the Guru. If you practice even this much, there will come a time when your life will be blessed with everything profound and good.

May all beings be blessed by the Guru's wisdom and compassion and may they attain the citadel of perfect enlightenment!

THE EXTRAORDINARY PRELIMINARY PRACTICE OF TAKING REFUGE

from the Pema Sangtig Ngondro

Taking refuge is the first step in the extraordinary preliminary practices of ngondro. You visualize the refuge tree according to the lineage. In the space before you, imagine an enormous mandala filled with beautiful flowers and abundant offerings of gold, silver, diamonds, trees, and mountains.

Then, in the center of this mandala, visualize a lotus flower. On the lotus flower is a moon disk. On that moon disk is Vajrasattva, the embodiment of all the buddhas of limitless time. Vajrasattva is lustrous white in color, and holds a vajra in his right hand and a bell in his left. Vajrasattva, as your root Guru, is embracing his luminous consort, who has a skull cup in her left hand and a hooked knife in her right hand. Surrounding the entire mandala is an ocean of dakas and dakinis.

Now, visualize yourself, your parents, and all sentient beings without exception bowing down and prostrating to this refuge mandala of Lama Vajrasattva. You and all sentient beings are paying respect, honoring Vajrasattva as your Lama with body, speech, and mind, and taking outer, inner, secret, and innermost secret refuge in the Lama and his retinue.

This Dzogchen ngondro is so profound that when your visualization is complete, not only are you doing prostrations and taking refuge, but all other sentient beings, without exception, bow to your enlightened teacher and take refuge in this golden lineage.

Even though in the refuge prayer you say, "I take refuge," you visualize that all sentient beings are saying this with you, "I take refuge." Therefore, "I" refers not solely to you but to all sentient beings. Your teacher is not an ordinary teacher but the embodiment of all the past, present, and future buddhas, and the refuge for all sentient beings. So, this refuge visualization is very clear, straightforward, and at the same time, very profound.

So, when you have established this visualization as clearly as you can, begin the prostrations, combining one prostration with one recitation of the refuge prayer as it is translated from the *Pema Sangtig* ngondro text:

Namo! The innate nature is primordially pure.
The expression is uncompounded luminosity.
You are the absolute deity, free from transformation
and change.
In the continuum of nonduality, I take refuge in you.

You have already taken outer, inner, and secret refuge when taking refuge in this profound lineage. You have taken outer refuge in the Buddha, Dharma, and Sangha; you have taken inner refuge in the lama, yidam, and dakini; and you have taken secret refuge in the three kayas: dharmakaya, sambhogakaya, and nirmanakaya. These three refuges include the innermost secret refuge of essence, nature, and compassion.

The first line of the refuge prayer states, "The innate nature is primordially pure." Primordial purity is natural and arises spontaneously; it cannot be made pure by anyone. Therefore, it is unconditional. The innate nature is primordially pure because that is how it is—that is its essence. In the Dzogchen tradition, *kadag* is the term for primordial purity, meaning "pure from the beginning," and the nature of that essence is *lhundrup*, meaning "spontaneously accomplished."

And what is the expression of this nature? The expression is uncompounded luminosity, which means it is free from obscurations. It is bright and luminous. Its expression is clarity. One cannot conceptualize it, nor can one point to it or grasp it. However, it can be experienced because it is our true nature.

When one takes refuge in the essence of primordial purity, self-arising luminosity is one's root Lama in the form of Vajrasattva.

You might wonder how compassion manifests in the form of the deity when you take refuge in this primordial purity. In this profound way of taking refuge, you perceive primordial purity as the essence of all that exists, and you see the expression of primordial purity, uncompounded luminosity, appearing as the display or deity in all that exists. Therefore, there is no room for duality, ignorance, or mental afflictions. There is no justification for hatred or jealousy. There is no benefit to being aggressive or greedy. There's no need to put things down or raise them up. In a sense, when you take refuge, all thought, activity, and experience is completely legitimized by understanding the uncompounded essence, that everything that appears is appearing out of this inexhaustible essence and nature. This is the greatest and most perfect way of understanding.

Of course, this is easier said than done. One must commit and take refuge with the conviction that nothing is more meaningful than freeing oneself from the suffering of cyclic existence. If it were as easy to do as to say, then you would not need to seek refuge in the Lama's wisdom. You would not require any help or guidance from the Lama. You would not need to recognize the primordially pure essence and nature of all that is, because you would already be experiencing it. You would be living in a state of natural primordial purity. You would be a living buddha.

However, when this is not the case, you do not experience the primordial purity of all that is. As a responsible human being, you must take the first step in the extraordinary practice of taking refuge in your true nature. You must take shelter in what is uncompounded, what is unelaborated, what is self-originated, what is independent, what is not conditional or tangible, what cannot be grasped by the intellect, and what cannot be fully expressed in words or thought.

To remain in the continuum of non-dual awareness and consistently recognize the primordially pure essence and reality of all that is, you must live each moment free from the ego's concept of the so-called structural self. To clarify all your thoughts, ideas, interactions, and everything that manifests in this world, you must remain in an unwavering state of selflessness, free from the self and not bound by dualistic thinking.

If you can remain in non-dual awareness while prostrating, you will hear the sound of countless beings prostrating and taking refuge along with you. Your devotion to the Lama and your prostrations will be so powerful and effective that the sound of innumerable sentient beings prostrating and reciting along with you will be louder than a thunderstorm. This is not impossible!

Why? Because there is no "I" in the state of nonduality to separate you from the rest of the world. There are no walls, doors, or fences. You must perform prostrations in this profound way. You must take refuge in this profound way. It will not be difficult to accomplish one hundred thousand prostrations because you will not work against the number. The ego will not fight against your commitment. If you are doing prostrations in this profound way, you should not feel pain in your knees, nor become exhausted after one, two, or three hours of prostrations. Prostrations will be like a dance for you, and you will dance with all the immeasurable beings in the universe. The last two lines of the refuge prayer read:

You are the absolute deity, free from transformation and change.
In the continuum of nonduality, I take refuge in you.

Now, why is the deity free from transformation and change? The deity is free from transformation and change because, without the ego's construction of self, there is nothing to change; there is no one to be changed; there is nothing to transform and no transformation that needs to happen. The deity itself is primordially pure clarity. From the beginning, the deity is indestructible. Therefore, this is the absolute deity; this is primordial purity; this is the luminosity.

Taking refuge in your root Lama in this way is the most profound way to go for refuge. As mentioned in the *Pema Sangtig* text, remember the refuge visualization you created in the sky above you when performing prostrations. Maintain that visualization while you prostrate.

When you create the mandala above you for the refuge practice, visualize earnestly with deep devotion and renunciation. Offer your heart to the Lama, and pay respect with body, speech, and mind. When giving your heart to the Lama, you honor the Lama. You become a deserving vessel to receive the inexhaustible nectar of the Lama's blessing.

Visualize this mandala of your root Lama with all the luminous deities, buddhas, bodhisattvas, dakas, and dakinis, both peaceful and wrathful. Visualize the mandala as vast as the universe. From that enormous mandala, white luminous light is shining throughout the universe.

Visualize that the white luminous light dissolves into you and purifies all your misdeeds and obscurations, and you are now without grasping to your ordinary body, speech, and mind. You dissolve into light—luminously pure vajra body, speech, and mind. This light, and the light of the entire retinue, dissolves into your root Lama. Now, you can no longer see or focus on the Lama, who also dissolves into insubstantial, radiant light.

This refuge practice is unimaginably powerful and inexpressible in words. It evokes a feeling of unlimited potential, as if anything could happen and everything is possible. It goes beyond your ordinary conception of what can or cannot occur. In amazement, it surpasses the ordinary mind, so to speak, with no grasping or attachment.

When you finish your prostrations, conclude with the dissolution of your visualization in this way:

From the field of refuge come rays of luminosity,
Dissolving into myself and all beings, obscurations are purified, melting into light,
Which dissolves into the field of refuge; the retinue is gath ered into the chief figure.
Even without this contrived visualization, remain in the unelaborated state.

Remain in this relaxed state of unelaborated samadhi for as long as you can.

THE EXTRAORDINARY PRELIMINARY PRACTICE OF BODHICHITTA

from the Pema Sangtig Ngondro

The second part of the extraordinary preliminary practice is establishing the mind in bodhichitta. When you understand what has been explained in the section on taking refuge, the bodhichitta practice will become clear to you. I have already explained the Dzogchen view of primordial purity, refuge, and visualization. Now, we are ready to focus on the bodhichitta practice, the generation of compassionate mind.

The generation of compassionate mind has two aspects. The first is to develop the wish to benefit sentient beings. The second is to begin practicing the bodhisattva path through compassionate action. These are the two general ways to cultivate bodhichitta. In the *Pema Sangtig* text, the bodhichitta recitation begins:

Ho! In the state of same taste, the great self-realization,
deluded beings appear without existing....

If you understand primordial purity, you realize that in the unconditional nature, deluded beings do not inherently exist. Within the state of primordial purity, all beings appear as luminous deities. If every being is a deity, how can there be deluded beings? Out of ignorance, deluded beings appear conditionally, without truly existing.

If you understand primordial purity, you realize that in the unconditional nature, deluded beings do not inherently exist. Within the state of primordial purity, all beings appear as luminous deities. If every being is a deity, how can there be deluded beings? Deluded beings appear without existing because they have not attained self-awareness, the state of "same taste," or great equanimity. Deluded beings have yet to recognize this fundamental state of primordial purity and, as a result, have impure perceptions.

However, there are no deluded beings in the state of great self-realization. Now, thanks to the teacher's kindness, blessings, and instructions, you can recognize your actual state of basic goodness. You wish to achieve this state and guide everyone toward this ultimate joy and freedom. Not only do all beings deserve to be in this state, but you also understand that this originally pure state is the intrinsic nature of all beings. Deluded beings are deluded only because they do not recognize or experience this primordially pure nature. They fail to see it due to the obscurations of dualistic perceptions, negative karma, and mental afflictions.

So, what should you do? By practicing this profound path, you must be determined to place all beings in the primordial state of wisdom. With this determination, you recite:

Ho! In the state of same taste, the great self-realization,
deluded beings appear without existing.
However, by the blessing of great secret means,
I will place everyone in primordial wisdom space.

"By the blessing of great secret means" refers to practicing this profound path of non-duality, the great equanimity, which frees you from ego and selfishness. When you recite this prayer, you must be fiercely determined to liberate all beings lost in darkness. With conviction, you recite, "I will place everyone in primordial wisdom space."

At the end of the recitation, remain in the state of equanimity and dedicate the virtue of this unconditional state to all sentient beings. The text concludes:

Saying this, accumulate the count and dedicate the virtue at the end of the session.

You dedicate the essence and virtue of your bodhichitta practice to all beings.

The meaning of this bodhichitta prayer is profound. The more you recite it quietly and sincerely, the deeper it penetrates. This is not a shallow practice, and it has no end. May we all give birth to hearts of compassion for the sake of all sentient beings!

THE EXTRAORDINARY PRELIMINARY PRACTICE OF VAJRASATTVA

from the Pema Sangtig Ngondro

The third extraordinary preliminary practice is Vajrasattva, which involves purification through meditation, visualization, and recitation of the Vajrasattva mantra.

In the refuge practice, there is a specific visualization, while in the bodhichitta practice, there is none. Here, in Vajrasattva you experience a sense of amazement and become immersed in the experience of "same taste," the great primordial purity. Now, you establish the visualization:

AH!
Above this ordinary form, on the crown of my head,
Is the wisdom form of all the Buddhas,
The glorious Guru Vajrasattva,
Radiant white and holding a vajra and bell,
Resting evenly in the self-luminous consort.
At the heart center on a moon disc, visualize the
seed-syllable HUM,
Circled by the mantra garland.
From the mantra mala of enlightened mind and body,

Vajrasattva

Continuously rain amrita light rays,
Which enter from the top of one's head,
Purifying all obscurations and sins, evil forces, and any sickness of the body.
Oneself is transformed into clear luminous light.

Above the crown of your head, your glorious root teacher appears as the embodiment of all the wisdom buddhas, taking the form of Vajrasattva, luminous white with a radiant luster, holding a vajra and a bell. He embraces his consort, who wields a hooked knife and a skull cup. At the center of Vajrasattva's heart, on a moon disk, visualize the seed syllable HUNG. Circling the letter HUNG is a garland, or mala, composed of the hundred-syllable mantra of Vajrasattva.

Visualize nectar descending from the seed syllable HUNG and the hundred-syllable mantra. You can imagine the nectar as clear liquid, or more profoundly, as luminous rays of light. Either way, these rays enter through the top of your head and fill your entire body with radiant light, cleansing and purifying all your sicknesses, troubles, negative thoughts, unwholesome deeds, and obscurations. The luminous nectar purifies everything within you, leaving you thoroughly cleansed. Visualize yourself bathed in this light; there is no negativity or darkness within you.

Here, as in the refuge practice with Vajrasattva, you also experience a sense of wonderment, immersed in the experience of "same taste." While visualizing Vajrasattva's luminous light nectar raining down on you and purifying all your obscurations and negativities, recite the hundred-syllable mantra of Vajrasattva (the English translation for its meaning is included):

OM

Is the supreme praise.

VAJRA SATTVA SA MA YA

The Vajrasattva samayas.

MA NU PA LA YA VAJRA SATTVA

Grant your protection Vajrasattva.

TE NO PA TISTA DRI DHO ME BHA WA

Remain firm in me.

SU TO KA YO ME BHA WA

Make me satisfied.

SU PO KA YO ME BHA WA

Increase the positive within me.

ANU RAKTO ME BHA WA

Be loving towards me.

SARVA SIDDHI ME PRA YATSA

Bestow all the accomplishments.

SARVA KARMA SU TSA ME

As well as all the activities.

TSITAM SHRE YAM KU RU

Make my mind virtuous!

HUM

Is the heart essence seed syllable.

HA HA HA HA

Symbolizes the four boundless qualities, four empowerments, four joys, and four kayas.

HO

Is the sound of joyous laughter in them.

BHA GA WAN SARVA TA THA GA TA
Bhagawan, all the Tathagatas

VAJRA MA ME MUNTSA
Vajrasattva don't abandon me.

VAJRI BHA WA
I pray I may become a vajra holder.

MA HA SA MA YA SATTVA
Great Samaya Sattva!

AH
Signifies uniting in non-duality.

As you visualize Guru Vajrasattva, understand that Vajrasattva represents the state of your true self and the state of your Lama.

The Guru Vajrasattva, greatly pleased, melts into light.
Dissolving into self, and oneself also
Radiates in the form of Vajrasattva, appearance inseparable with emptiness.

Here again, the idea that there is an "I" that exists as something conditional and concrete dissolves because you are now purified of all duality. You appear, but that appearance is inseparable from emptiness. Since the appearance is inseparable from emptiness, there is no inherently existing self. There is nothing to grasp or hold to. Remain in that state of meditation. The text says:

Visualizing, as said above, recite the six-syllable mantra.

So, with the visualization in which one has been completely purified and rests in the form of Vajrasattva, appearance inseparable from emptiness, recite the six-syllable mantra as much as possible:

OM VAJRASATTVA HUNG

Then,

Rest in the continuum of the natural state, unfabricated mind.

THE EXTRAORDINARY PRELIMINARY PRACTICE OF MANDALA OFFERING

from the Pema Sangtig Ngondro

The fourth section of the extraordinary preliminary practice is the mandala offering.

It is amazing how each ngondro practice seamlessly follows the next. Now that you are purified through Vajrasattva practice, the external world is also purified. Whatever exists in this world and the universe is worth offering to the Lama because you appreciate and cherish its beauty. Offer the external world of magnificent mountains, valleys, oceans, rivers, earth, and sky.

The mandala offering begins:

OM AH HUM
I offer this external vessel, the mandala of the universe,
Filled with supreme qualities of gods and humans
To you, nirmanakaya Lama.

You offer the external world to the nirmanakaya Lama because it is what you have, and you can only offer what you have. Because you are purified, you see that the external world is perfect as it is. There is nothing wrong with this world; it is not imperfect. So, offer everything in this world to the nirmanakaya Lama. What you create in your mind exists within your imagination. You can imagine the pure land of Guru Padmasambhava, filled with everything precious. This would be worthy of offering. With this vast understanding, offer this mandala of the universe to the Nirmanakaya Lama. Then the text reads:

I offer this body, the vessel of the mandala,
Adorned with the radiance of elements and faculties
To you, sambhogakaya Lama.

You have your body along with all its senses. Through your body and senses, you can experience everything in this world. So, with deep reverence and gratitude, dedicate your body and your sense faculties of sight, sound, smell, taste, and touch to the Sambhogakaya Lama. Then:

I offer this mandala of clear empty space,
Adorned with the ornament of unobstructed awakened awareness
To you, dharmakaya Lama.

The unobstructed awakened awareness you offer to the Lama in this mandala offering is the state of dharmakaya, as explained in the section on the extraordinary preliminary refuge. You offer this primordially pure state to the dharmakaya Lama.

Why do you make offerings to the dharmakaya, sambhogakaya, and nirmanakaya Lamas? There are no separate dharmakaya, sambhogakaya, or nirmanakaya Lamas. All three kayas exist simultaneously within your root Lama. Then why do you make each offering separately, when they are inseparable? You offer the outer, inner, and secret offerings separately to acknowledge everything you have or could imagine, without missing anything. You offer all you have by recognizing the three kayas—the essence, the nature, and the compassionate energy. However, in the awareness of nowness, these three kayas are inseparable. The text continues:

May the three realms, this universe and inhabitants,
be self-liberated,
And may the pure field of the three kayas be realized!

How are the three realms self-liberated? Self-liberation is only possible if you realize your true self-nature as the inseparability of the three kayas. In this higher teaching, we use the term primordial purity rather than emptiness to describe the ultimate nature of mind. In this higher view, the essence is primordially pure, the nature is spontaneously accomplished, and the energy is the unobstructed flow of compassion. You liberate this universe and its inhabitants by fully realizing and actualizing this profound view.

Your contrived actions do not liberate this universe and its inhabitants. Rather, you pray that the universe and its inhabitants will be effortlessly self-liberated. For example, when clouds go away, we see the sun shining. When clouds cover the sun, it seems like the sun isn't shining. But this isn't true. The sun is always shining. The sun's rays are naturally self-liberated when the wind blows and the clouds dissipate. No one needs to do anything to free the sun's brightness. The sun's light is self-liberated.

Nevertheless, one who has not yet achieved self-realization and primordial purity must work to dispel the darkness of obscuration by gathering merit. The mandala offering is a way to gather merit, and by completing the mandala offering one hundred thousand times, it is possible to purify everything and realize the pure field of the sacred mandala. When realizing the pure field, one manifests the dharmakaya, sambhogakaya, and nirmanakaya, not only for oneself but for all sentient beings, and one experiences the pure land of buddha. For one's own benefit and that of all sentient beings, one accumulates merit through the mandala offering.

The text closes with the mantra of mandala offering:

OM AH HUNG SARVA GURU MANDALA PUJA MEGHA AH HUNG

OM is the essence of the kayas of all past, present, and future buddhas. AH is the essence of the speech of all past, present, and future buddhas. And HUNG is the essence of the mind and heart of all past, present, and future buddhas. SARVA means all, or limitless. GURU means precious one, or mother of compassion. MANDALA means creation. PUJA means offering. MEGHA AH HUNG means offering to fulfill one's wishes and accumulate merit. With that mantra recitation you finish the mandala offering.

So, you recite the entire mandala offering from the beginning:

OM AH HUM
I offer this external vessel, the mandala of the universe,
Filled with supreme qualities of gods and humans
To you, nirmanakaya Lama.
I offer this body, the vessel of the mandala,
Adorned with the radiance of elements and faculties
To you, sambhogakaya Lama
I offer this mandala of clear empty space,
Adorned with the ornament of unobstructed awakened awareness
To you, dharmakaya Lama.

May the three realms, this universe, and its inhabitants
be self-liberated,
and may the pure field of the three kayas be realized!

OM AH HUNG SARVA GURU MANDALA PUJA MEGHA AH HUNG

At the end of the mandala offering, all realms of desire, form, and formlessness, along with the universe as the vessel and all inhabitants within it, by self-liberation through the accumulation of merit, will attain and realize the buddhafield of indestructible body, speech, and mind, which is the pure field of inseparable nirmanakaya, sambhogakaya, and dharmakaya.

THE EXTRAORDINARY PRELIMINARY PRACTICE OF GURU YOGA

from the Pema Sangtig Ngondro

Please listen to the teachings of Guru Yoga with genuine trust and pure devotion. Strive for perfect enlightenment for yourself and for the benefit of all sentient beings.

First, imagine a vast, pure realm filled with rainbows and spheres of five-colored lights. In front of you, visualize a sun and moon disk hovering above a lotus flower. Sitting on these disks is your root Guru, who demonstrates the triple kindness by giving you teachings, instructions, and empowerment. Therefore, the Guru's kindness is immeasurable.

Your root Guru is in the form of deathless Padmasambhava. He is brightly glowing, with a beautiful smile, and is adorned with all good qualities. He wears a lotus crown. Sitting with crossed legs in the vajra posture, he is dressed in the ornaments and attire of the perfected nine yanas.

To practice Guru Yoga perfectly, you see your Guru as none other than a buddha in person. The more you see your Guru as a buddha, the more swiftly and effectively you will receive the blessings of this practice.

In Guru Padmasambhava's heart center, visualize the blissful, indestructible Amitayus. Amitayus is white, with a luminous luster, and holds a deathless longevity vase in his two hands. He is united with his radiant consort, the union of bliss and emptiness.

Externally, the entire mandala is encircled with five-colored lights. The eight great Vidyadhara *siddhas*, and an ocean of yogis circle as the external retinue. These deities are in samadhi, the state of great equanimity, appearance inseparable from emptiness.

When this visualization has been stabilized, recite the seven-line prayer:

HUNG!
On the northwest border of the country of Uddiyana,
On the anthers of a lotus flower,
You attained the marvelous supreme siddhi.
Renowned as the Lotus Born,
Surrounded by a retinue of many dakinis,
Following in your footsteps, I will practice.
Please come and grant your blessings!
GURU PADMA SIDDHI HUNG!

By reciting the seven-line prayer, you invoke your root Guru, who appears as Padmasambhava.

Then recite the seven-branch offering:

OM AH HUM!
To the assembly of deathless, long-life deities,
I prostrate respectfully to the great pure equanimity.
I present clouds of offerings, of the union of senses
and objects.
I confess ignorant delusion into space.
I will rejoice in the profound non-conceptual state.
Please turn the wheel of the great symbolic blissful Dharma.
I pray that you remain in the great state

of non-transformation.
I dedicate all merits to the youthful vase body.

At the beginning of the ngondro, you recite the four points that turn the mind to Dharma: the preciousness of this human life, impermanence, cause and effect, and the defects of samsara. Then, at the end of the ngondro, you do this Guru Yoga practice, which includes this seven-branch offering:

To the assembly of deathless, long-life deities,
I prostrate respectfully to the great pure equanimity.

You prostrate and respectfully pay homage to your root Guru, Guru Padmasambhava, to the entire retinue, and all the buddhas and bodhisattvas who dwell in the state of primordial purity. When you prostrate and recite this seven-branch offering, there is no duality. You rest in a state of great equanimity.

I present clouds of offerings, of the union of senses
and objects.

In this state of great equanimity, the sense faculties and sense objects are united. For instance, when you drink tea, the drinker, the tea you drink, and the drinking itself are inseparable. You do not necessarily have to take your tea to the altar and offer it to the deities. Realizing the primordially pure state, and remaining in this state of great equanimity, everything you do becomes an offering.

When you buy and wear a new shirt for the first time, you offer it to the Guru. When you comb your hair, that is an offering to the Guru. When you shower, cleansing your body is an offering to the Guru. When you wake up and see a beautiful sunrise, you offer it to the Guru. There is no grasping and no desire to possess anything for yourself. Your entire life becomes an offering.

One deludes oneself by using concepts to label and possess things. Then, after following one thought after the other, there is confusion and uncertainty. One confuses oneself. You become ignorant of your true nature. This entanglement of thoughts is the suffering of samsara. You do not recognize how your habitual thoughts cause more and more confusion. You do not see that everything arises and dissolves into emptiness.

I confess ignorant delusion into space.

Whatever negativity, confusion, or delusion you have created in your mind, you confess into emptiness. Here, confession means to purify, to be free of. When you understand emptiness all your ignorance and delusion disappear, and you are free of them. You go back to the natural source, back to your original place.

I will rejoice in the profound non-conceptual state.

Realizing the profound view that frees you from suffering, you rejoice. You see your true nature, inexpressible and beyond conception.

Please turn the wheel of the great symbolic blissful Dharma.

You joyfully request the Guru to turn the wheel of the great symbolic blissful Dharma so that all sentient beings, including yourself, will be free from suffering.

I pray that you remain in the great state of non-transformation.

Since that realization is free from transformation and change, you request that your Guru remain in the state of emptiness and luminous clarity, free from transformation and change.

I dedicate all merit to the youthful vase body.

You dedicate your merit to the youthful vase body—the nonconceptual space of emptiness. You dedicate your merit by remaining in this state beyond conditional duality.

The seven-branch prayer expresses profound devotion to your root Guru, to Padmasambhava, and to the entire lineage. When you are with the Guru, always be mindful. The Guru embodies the perfectly enlightened state. If you can see this quality in the Guru, you begin to see it in yourself. You pray that your mind and the Guru's mind become inseparable. You see that the Guru is a wish-fulfilling jewel. You see your Guru and Padmasambhava as your only hope in the world.

After making offerings, you pray to the Guru, requesting ordinary and extraordinary blessings:

To Guru Rinpoche, the embodiment of all buddhas,
embodiment of the triple kindness, root Guru,
I pray one-pointedly, with intense heartfelt longing.
Please grant ordinary and extraordinary accomplishments.

Ordinary accomplishments refer to everything you can understand conceptually and achieve in the relative world. Extraordinary accomplishments refer to profound, exponential, luminous wisdom that is inconceivable and beyond conception. You pray to Padmasambhava and your root Guru to grant you both ordinary and extraordinary accomplishments. The Guru kindly gives you teachings, instructions, and empowerment. You pray to your root teacher without the slightest doubt, without a second thought, from the bottom of your heart, for the ordinary and extraordinary accomplishments. From the Guru's four places, the forehead, throat, heart, and navel centers, visualize luminous rays of light descending instantaneously, cleansing and purifying all your obscurations and misdeeds.

From the Guru's four places—the forehead, throat, heart, and navel chakras, the energy centers of the subtle body—visualize luminous rays of light descending instantaneously, cleansing and purifying all your obscurations and misdeeds.

From the Guru's forehead, visualize rays of white light entering your forehead. Through this, the physical non-virtues and obscurations of the body are purified, and you receive the blessing of the indestructible vajra body.

From the Guru's throat center, visualize a flash of red light entering your throat. Through this, the non-virtues and obscurations of speech are purified, and you receive the blessing of meaningfully eloquent vajra speech.

From the heart center of the Guru, visualize a sapphire blue light entering your heart center, purifying all non-virtue and the obscurations of the mind. Your creative essence or energy is purified, and you receive the blessing of luminous vajra mind.

Finally, from the navel center of the Guru, rays of light of the five colors—white, red, blue, yellow, and green dissolve into your navel center, purifying all subtle defilements and obscurations arising from the substrate consciousness. You receive the blessing of blissful vajra wisdom and are empowered to meditate on Dzogchen, the Great Perfection.

After these four self-empowerments, visualize the entire retinue surrounding your Guru dissolving into light. This light, in turn, dissolves into your root Guru. Then your root Guru, the embodiment of all the buddhas of the three times, is pleased and dissolves into you. Remain in deep samadhi with no dualistic ideas—no thoughts of good or bad, no concepts of pure or impure, perfect or imperfect. Remain in the continuum of the natural state of unfabricated mind.

Then, conclude by dedicating the merit of this practice to all sentient beings.

This virtue and other virtues, by binding all into one,
I dedicate to the space of inexhaustible dharmakaya.
May we obtain buddhahood without meeting or separating.

Praying to Padmasambhava, who is inseparable from your root Guru, is the supreme practice for gathering blessings and swiftly attaining enlightenment. I encourage you to practice Guru Yoga with heartfelt devotion.

His Eminence Shyalpa Rinpoche's Reading & Oral Commentary on

EXTRACTING THE QUINTESSENCE OF ACCOMPLISHMENT: INSTRUCTIONS FOR PRACTICING MOUNTAIN RETREAT

by His Holiness Dudjom Rinpoche

The teaching is *Extracting the Quintessence of Accomplishment: Instructions for Practicing Mountain Retreat* by His Holiness Dudjom Rinpoche. Please listen carefully, as these teachings are profound and vital for your practice.

Dudjom Rinpoche begins by paying homage to the Guru, whose kindness is unmatched. He prays for the Guru's blessings so that realization quickly arises within himself and his disciples, enabling them all to reach the citadel of the primordial ground.

One pays homage to the Guru with genuine devotion and gratitude. The Guru embodies primordially pure awareness, the ultimate ground of all beings. With genuine reverence and respect, one becomes a worthy vessel for these profound teachings of the Great Perfection.

For those who have accumulated merit and for those whose karma has ripened, for those who have devotion and confidence in the Guru and in the Great Perfection, and for those who wish to complete the practice in this lifetime, Dudjom Rinpoche explains the essence of the practice of mountain retreat.

The text has three main topics:

First, the preparation: Cutting through compulsive attachment and purifying the mind of obscurations and afflictions.

Second, the main practice: Eliminating doubts about view, meditation, and conduct, and accomplishing the practice.

Third, keeping commitments: Upholding your commitments in post-meditation and embodying the Dharma in all your actions.

FIRST TOPIC

The Preparation: releasing attachment and purifying the mind

Dudjom Rinpoche begins by expressing sadness: "Alas, our so-called mind has arisen simultaneously with Samantabhadra." Samantahbadra means always good and always pure. Samantabhadra is the original buddha, the basic goodness of enlightened awareness. Although the original mind is always good, we are still in ignorance.

We are here, unaware of our true nature, and so we are constantly moving, wandering in samsara. For countless lifetimes, we take birth in the six realms: the human realm, the god realm, the jealous god realm, the animal realm, the hungry ghost realm, and the hell realm. As we endlessly wander through the confusion of these six realms, everything we do ultimately lacks meaning. This is a cause for deep sorrow.

This life in the human realm is just one of countless lives. If we don't use this human life wisely, we will keep being reborn in samsara. We can't know where we'll be born next. Being born as a human isn't enough; we need to grasp the importance of this precious human life. Everything that is born is impermanent and will decay. The time of death is unknown. So, we must practice urgently right now! Like the great yogi Milarepa, we will have no regrets and not be ashamed of ourselves at the time of death.

We practice the Dharma to transform the mind, cutting through our attachments to this life. We question the things that we believe are essential: a luxurious home, a beautiful car, and a successful career. It is not enough to adopt the façade of a pious practitioner; we need to look inward and cut through the habits that bind us to samsara. Our clinging acts as the primary cause and the objects of attachment as the contributing conditions, creating obstacles to spiritual growth, and we continue to behave in ignorant, mundane ways.

So, how should we practice? We should care less about delicious food and fashionable clothing. We should cut back on meaningless talk and useless gossip. We should reduce all of our attachments. Then we can focus our minds one-pointedly on practice.

The great enlightened one Gyalwa Yang Gonpa said, "In a lonely place, with awareness of death fixed in the heart, the practitioner, deeply disgusted with attachments, draws the boundaries of the retreat by renouncing concerns for this life, and does not meet with the eight worldly concerns."

The eight worldly concerns are gain and loss, pleasure and pain, praise and blame, and fame and obscurity. We want to gain; we don't want loss. We like pleasure; we don't want pain. We like praise; we don't want blame. We want fame; we don't want obscurity.

Dudjom Rinpoche says to be like the great yogi, Gyalwa Yang Gonpa, disgusted with attachments and worldly concerns.

Attachment and aversion are like demons—obstacles that impede one's spiritual growth. Without diligently practicing Dharma, these obstacles will never end. The eight worldly concerns give rise to attachment and aversion, which in turn lead to hope and fear. For example, take an expensive Rolex watch, which is stylish, desirable, and costly. You desire the watch and hope to possess it. But you can't afford it, and that creates frustration. The watch becomes an object of your attachment and aversion.

Dudjom Rinpoche counsels us to let go of our attachment to home and the motherland. We often cling to our family, community, and country. Let go of these ties and wander in unknown places. Don't obsess about your family's reputation or wealth. You accomplish half of the Dharma by leaving your country or motherland behind.

In Western cultures, children are expected to leave their parents' home when they become adults. However, this does not mean that they have accomplished half of the Dharma. Accomplishing half of the Dharma means renouncing the eight worldly concerns. This is what it means to leave your home. The eight worldly concerns proliferate when clinging to your homeland.

Don't listen to those who try to discourage you from practicing the Dharma. Your parents want you to be happy, but they don't understand the true source of happiness. They think that friends, wealth, success, and status bring happiness. However, this only leads to more attachment and aversion. Never satisfied with what you have, you become a slave to the demons of desire.

Don't be concerned about what people say. Don't care about kind words or harsh words. Don't care about praise or blame. Let people say whatever they want as if they were talking to someone dead and buried. Listen with the ear of a corpse.

Only your Guru can offer sound advice about the Dharma. Farm animals are linked to a rope by a ring through their noses and led by their masters. Dudjom Rinpoche says, "Do not hand your nose-rope to others," meaning don't let others turn your head this way and that. To practice Dharma, you need principles and integrity. If someone tries to hinder or discourage your practice, be immovable, like an iron boulder being pulled by a silk scarf. Don't be weak and noncommittal, bending your head in whatever direction the wind blows, like grass on a mountain path. To have principles doesn't mean you oppose others; it means having the courage of your convictions.

Dudjom Rinpoche says, "Whatever practice you do, from the moment you begin until you reach the ultimate end, whether thunder and lightning fall from above, a lake springs from below, or rocks fall on all sides, having sworn not to break your promise even at the cost of your life, you should persevere until the end."

When you decide to practice, your commitment has to be rock-solid, especially during a strict retreat. Once you commit to practicing Dharma, you persevere. If you cannot practice in an isolated retreat, at the very least, don't spend your time engaging in gossip, negative thoughts, or unwholesome behavior.

Practice a strict outer, inner, and secret retreat. Outer retreat is practicing Dharma day and night alone in an isolated place. You don't go outside to entertain yourself. The inner retreat is keeping to your practice without giving in to distractions. And secret retreat is maintaining awareness, not wavering for a moment, like a peg driven deep in the ground.

For the purification of body, speech, and mind, there are the common preliminaries—the four points that turn the mind to Dharma: the rarity of precious human birth, the truth of impermanence and the certainty of death, the infallible nature of karma, and the suffering of samsara.

The uncommon preliminaries of the mahayana and vajrayana are taking refuge in Buddha, Dharma, and Sangha; cultivating bodhichitta, the aspiration to become enlightened for the benefit of all sentient beings; purifying all obstacles and obscurations; and accumulating merit and wisdom. Above all, practice Guru yoga, union with the Guru's enlightened body, speech, and mind. This is the heart of your practice. Dudjom Rinpoche says, "If you pray with simple and fervent devotion, merging your mind with the mind of the Guru, an extraordinary and inexpressible understanding will arise from within."

Today, pure devotion is very rare. Ultimately, the blessings you receive depend on the strength of your faith and devotion to the Guru. It is said that only a pure vessel can receive blessings. In the Himalayas, it was believed that the snow lion's milk had to be stored in a golden vessel or else it would spoil or leak out. To receive the Guru's direct transmission of the snow lion's milk, your devotion must be as pure as gold. The extraordinary preliminary practices will forge a golden vessel, making you a suitable vessel for direct transmission, the heart-mind realization of the Guru. This is why I encourage my students to practice the preliminaries.

Lama Zhang Rinpoche said many practitioners focus on cultivating stillness, samadhi, and other practices. But rare is the realization that arises from within, due to the Guru's powerful blessings, born of trust and devotion.

SECOND TOPIC

The Main Practice: view, meditation, and conduct

View

In Dzogchen, the Great Perfection, the practice involves view, meditation, and conduct. Dudjom Rinpoche emphasizes that the view is the realization of the nature of mind, the absolute nature of reality beyond all conceptual elaboration. The view is self-originated, naked, unconditional awareness. One begins with the view, a decisive recognition of the actual nature of mind itself.

We need to be careful here. There is a distinction between the ordinary mind and mind itself. The ordinary mind is the movement of thoughts, feelings, and perceptions, it holds opinions about right and wrong, it is always projecting, and this is the activity of a confused mind, not the true nature of mind itself. The true nature of mind is unborn, free from any basis or root. The essence of mind is unfabricated and unchanging. There is no rejection or acceptance—only pure, self-originated awareness.

The nature of mind itself is inconceivable. No example can describe it fully. Mind itself is not made worse by samsara, nor is it made better by nirvana. It is timelessly unchanging. Mind itself is not born and does not cease.

The mind of awareness itself is eternally pure and perfect, an all-pervading primordial purity. It is spacious, vast, and empty, yet also luminously clear. As the radiance of emptiness is unobstructed, all the possibilities of samsara and nirvana emerge. When awareness of nowness is realized, the sun of luminous clarity shines without end. The natural mind is like the sun, embodying the essence of the dharmakaya.

Appearance and emptiness are inseparable. This is the view. This view is beyond ordinary mind, beyond thought, beyond conception. Guru Padmasambhava said that the essence of dharmakaya is beyond the intellect. The intellect is ordinary mind, ordinary thought. The nature of mind itself is Dzogchen, the Great Perfection.

Years ago, I attended a barbecue at a Buddhist center in New Jersey. Everyone was having a good time enjoying the hot dogs and hamburgers, and there was plenty of beer. The guy who was serving food had too much to drink. He was rowdy and began to shout, "I am Buddha; I am Buddha! I have a Dzogchen hot dog! I have a Dzogchen hamburger! Who wants to eat? I have Dzogchen here."

I felt compassion for him. I approached him and poked him in the chest. "Where is your Dzogchen hamburger? I want to have it right now!" He was stunned. I asked him, "Who taught you this Dzogchen?" He muttered the name of his teacher. I said, "Don't blame your teacher. This is not the Dzogchen that a good Lama teaches."

We went to a quiet place where I spoke to him about Dzogchen. I explained how Dzogchen is a sacred and secret teaching. If you speak of it flippantly, you can create negative karma. We talked in a friendly way. He asked me if I would be his teacher. I said yes, if you practice Dzogchen sincerely, from your heart and not from your mouth.

In Dzogchen, there is always a danger of misunderstanding. We must understand the difference between the ordinary deluded mind and the nature of mind itself. The Great Perfection is profound and subtle. With understanding and sincere effort, you can accomplish everything.

Some of my Western students see themselves as serious practitioners who think they understand Dzogchen. They ask, "Why do we need to engage in preliminary practice? If the mind is already pure and perfect, why do we need to practice?" They fail to recognize that they have not yet transcended the dualistic mind of samsara. They have not yet realized the essence of mind itself. They don't see pristine awareness, mind as such.

The view is the principle of the Great Perfection, the essence of all the Buddha's teachings, and the essence of the tantras of Dzogchen. There is nothing more beyond this principle. This is the ultimate. When you recognize this, the ultimate nature of all phenomena, you have certainty in the view. You are free from all doubt.

Dudjom Rinpoche says, "What a wonder it is to behold in our hands Samantabhadra's wisdom mind! Samantabhadra represents the first buddha, the original buddha. How marvelous! How fortunate! We are touching the very heart, lungs, and marrow of Dzogchen!" This is the ultimate essence of the Lord Buddha's teachings. There is nothing beyond this view, the view of the Great Perfection!

Meditation

When you have certainty about the view and the unconditional nature of mind itself, sustain this view and remain in the continuum of awareness. With body, speech, and mind settled in the natural state, you remain relaxed and at ease. This is the meditation that is without distraction. If you meditate with an intention, with a target, this is not Dzogchen meditation. In the practice of Great Perfection, meditation is effortless non-meditation. If you are meditating to free yourself from suffering or attain enlightenment, this is not effortless non-meditation.

The path of the Great Perfection is not a religion. The pure, primordial nature of mind itself is beyond all dogmas and beliefs. In pure awareness, there is no distinction between race, religion, culture, or country. Wherever there is mind as such, there is non-dual purity. When there is perfect devotion and trust in the Guru, you can experience it for yourself. You have direct experience, but you couldn't fully express it. It's like trying to describe the taste of chocolate to someone who has never tasted it. The view of the Great Perfection is inexpressible and inconceivable. One has to be able to remain continuously in awareness of nowness, without any deliberate effort. If awareness is lost in discursive thoughts, that is not the practice of the Great Perfection.

Without losing the principle, without straying from the simplicity of the view, with confidence, remain relaxed and at ease. Let the perceptions of the five sense-doors release into their natural state. Do not meditate on any object, on any particular thing. Do not rely on antidotes. If you do, this is just ordinary practice and deluded thinking.

Remain free and relaxed while maintaining awareness. Do not be distracted for a single moment. Rest in a continuous state of unwavering awareness. When a thought arises, allow it to come and go without chasing after it. Remain innocently fresh and natural without grasping or holding on.

Dudjom Rinpoche says, "Well then, what should you do? Whatever appearances arise, be like a young child gazing around in a temple. All phenomena will remain in their own place. Their appearances are not modified, their colors do not change, and their luster doesn't fade. Phenomena appear, but they are not contaminated by grasping and attachment. All appearances will arise as naked pure appearances and radiant wisdom."

You dwell in the pure, intrinsic nature beyond fabrication. You throw away all of your clothing, so to speak; you have no fear of being naked before the world. Free of the fragile and insecure ego, you have nothing to hide. You have nothing to fear.

Don't fear this purity, this freedom. Are you afraid of losing your ego or sense of self? Who would you be without your cherished beliefs? This fear is unnecessary. Without clinging to the self, we become more fully alive. We see everything more clearly. At that moment, compassion for all beings grows vast, infinite, and all-encompassing.

The essence of Great Perfection is in the interval when past thoughts have ceased and future thoughts have not yet arisen. This perception of nowness is a bare freshness. This experience of nowness is beyond the three times of past, present, and future. Dudjom Rinpoche says, "Is this not a virgin, pristine, clear, awakened state of bare freshness that has never changed as much as a hair's breadth? Ah, how marvelous! This is awareness itself! If one does not continually remain in this state, doesn't a discursive thought suddenly arise? This is the creative expression of pure awareness itself. However, if you do not recognize it as soon as it arises and thoughts flow out in a steady stream, this is called 'the chain of delusion,' and it is the root of samsara. By recognizing thoughts as soon as they appear, if they are not allowed to proliferate, they are instantly released and liberated into the expanse of pure awareness—the dharmakaya. This is the main practice, in which the view and meditation of *trekchod*, or cutting through, are united."

Moment by moment, as thoughts arise, don't identify with them; recognize them as the pure energy display of mind itself. Meditation is remaining in this state of pure awareness and recognizing thoughts as the energetic display of the mind. This meditation is like the endless flow of a river. Both beautiful flowers and smelly trash float on the river. The river does not discriminate between them. But we accept the flowers and reject the trash. In the view of Great Perfection, once you are free of concepts and labels, both nirvana and samsara, good and bad, are equally empty of intrinsic existence.

On the path of Great Perfection, we leave the shore and leap into the natural course of the river. We move with the flow and swim with the energy. Pure awareness does not lapse into ordinary judgments of good or bad. We are free to roam and play in the open expanse of awareness.

Garab Dorje, the first human to elucidate the teachings of Great Perfection, said:

Mindfulness of the instant that pristine awareness arises,
From the very nature of primordially pure absolute space,
Is like finding a jewel in the depths of the ocean.
This is the dharmakāya, which is not contrived or created by anyone.

Conduct

The principal point is to see your teacher as an enlightened being, as a buddha. Sakyamuni Buddha himself said that there is no buddha before the Guru. Never for a single moment think of your Guru as an ordinary being. Pray from your heart with devotion. This is the universal panacea, the one medicine that cures all disease. This one practice is equivalent to countless other methods. Devotion is the supreme practice for dispelling obstacles and making progress on the spiritual path.

During meditation, if your mind becomes dull and lethargic, revive awareness with an alert sense of presence. If your mind becomes scattered and unruly, relax deeply from within. But do not apply force. There is no need to alter or control appearances. Let things be as they are—naked, fresh, clear, vast, and transparent. Thoughts will surface, but in all of this, there is nothing but the action of recognizing the natural state of awareness.

We are incredibly fortunate to have this profound practice! You are blessed if you can truly understand this view and then put it into practice. Many believe they can express this in words, but haven't experienced it firsthand. They become like parrots, just repeating empty words.

There is no need to meditate on a conceptual idea of emptiness as an antidote. When you recognize the true nature of thoughts, they dissolve instantly. The moment a thought arises, it immediately dissolves back into emptiness. All afflictions and obscurations self-liberate naturally. If you have a jealous thought, you don't need an antidote or a method to eliminate it. It's like a snake that doesn't need help to untie itself; it frees itself effortlessly.

After receiving these profound instructions on the swift path of Great Perfection, Dudjom Rinpoche says, "that if you don't put them into practice, it is like placing a wish-fulfilling jewel into the mouth of a corpse—it is totally useless! So, practice, and don't let your heart rot!"

There are two deadly enemies. We need to understand these two enemies: the apprehender and the apprehended. Dualistic fixation involves the subject that apprehends and the object that is apprehended. These are the most dangerous enemies. They are the root of suffering. We have developed nuclear weapons to kill our brothers and sisters, but bombs cannot destroy these two enemies. By the grace of the Guru, we are introduced to the nature of primordial purity—dharmakaya—which burns up these enemies. Dudjom Rinpoche says, "When you burn a feather, it leaves no residue. Isn't that satisfying?"

As a beginner, you will find your mind invaded by negative thoughts and stray into distraction. Subtle thoughts will proliferate unnoticed. Then, a lucid mindfulness returns, and you realize you have wandered. When the mind strays into distraction, do not try to interrupt the course of thoughts. Right at that moment, do not try to change anything and do not feel regret about wandering. Don't denigrate yourself, thinking you are naughty, dull, or stupid. Avoid settling into a quiet, sleepy state. Remain alert, looking directly at the thoughts without analyzing or pondering. Rest upon the "recognizer" of the thoughts, and don't give the thoughts any credence. Be like a grownup watching children at play, not taking their fantasy games seriously.

As you progress in meditation, you will experience periods of bliss, clarity, and non-thought. Do not cling to these fleeting experiences or try to sustain them. All conditioned experiences are fleeting; no matter how pleasant, they will fade. Whatever the experience, good or bad, don't grasp; remain undistracted. Discard distractions with constant, vigilant practice.

A few good meditation experiences are not enough. Some yogis take pride in their experiences and understanding, believing they have accomplished something significant. Small moments of clarity and bliss can deceive and confuse them. One must continuously refine one's meditation until they have a genuine realization beyond mere intellectual understanding. A little knowledge can lead to pride and arrogance, but conceptual understanding is temporary, like mist that disappears or a patch that wears off. You need to clarify your experience repeatedly. Otherwise, the profound instructions will remain in books, and no genuine meditation will arise.

Practice with great energy, day and night, without distraction. Dudjom Rinpoche says, "Do not allow emptiness to remain in the domain of theory, bring everything back to awareness itself. Don't let your intellect rule. If you do, you will deceive yourself!"

Some of my followers will express their desire to join our community and ask me how they can contribute. I tell them to meditate and do the preliminary practices, and as you deepen your practice, you will see all sentient beings as your mothers and fathers, brothers and sisters, and sons and daughters. Loving-kindness and compassion will blossom spontaneously, and your innate wisdom and self-awareness will show you the way.

Practicing meditation only occasionally is not sufficient. Without consistent practice, the mind becomes lazy and dull. I see some senior students who arrogantly belittle newcomers. These so-called senior students are busy and don't have time to meditate. I tell them to meditate and do the preliminary practices as Padmasambhava and all the Enlightened Ones have advised. When dying, foolish scholars who haven't practiced tremble and clutch their chests, while enlightened yogis relax in their final moments and depart this world peacefully.

Practice continuously until you reach the state of effortless non-meditation. Through continuous practice and devotion to the teacher over a long time, experiences transform into realization. With trust in the Guru, everything appears before you in a very beautiful way. In trying circumstances, you will not be afraid; you will be confident that you can handle everything.

In the snowy mountains of the Himalayas, the great yogis wore only a thin robe. They didn't care about pleasing others. They had one pot and one bowl and survived with almost nothing. The snow around a yogi's cave would melt from their inner heat. With their radiant bodies of pure awareness, they transformed internally, and outer conditions could not affect them.

Dudjom Rinpoche says, "This is like taking a covering off your head. What a happy relief!" This is the supreme seeing where nothing is seen. The Dzogchen yogi sees that his true nature is the one taste of emptiness, so there is nothing to see other than the inseparability of appearance and emptiness, bliss and emptiness. This is the extraordinary beauty that isn't seen only with the senses.

If you have this inner accomplishment, outer circumstances cannot harm you. Outwardly, my lineage masters appeared to be ordinary people—very simple and carefree. They dressed plainly and often avoided others. But inwardly, they were perfectly attuned to the true nature of all phenomena.

At first, thoughts are liberated through recognition, like meeting an old acquaintance you haven't seen in a long time. Then, after a while, thoughts naturally self-liberate, like the knots in a snake unraveling. Finally, thoughts are released without benefit or harm, like a thief entering an empty house. These occur gradually over time, and then there is a decisive recognition that all phenomena are the magical displays of self-awareness. There will be no way to choose between samsara and nirvana, and there will be no distinctions of good or bad regarding buddhas and sentient beings.

Although yogis and yoginis appear to be ordinary people, their minds dwell in the effortless dharmakaya. Without action, they traverse all levels and paths. When attaining enlightenment, your body doesn't transform into a deity with a crown of jewels and a golden glow. You do not ascend to a place beyond this magnificent and wondrous world. You drink from the same glass and eat off the same plate. You have the same face and figure. But you remain in the continuum of pure awareness and sublime bliss.

The fruition of the view, meditation, and action is not something one can grasp from outside. The fruit is only attainable from within, but one has to realize and actualize it in the moment. Direct experience and realization may happen gradually or instantaneously. It depends on one's karma and accumulation of merit and wisdom.

THIRD TOPIC

Keeping Commitments: applying the Dharma in daily life

The third topic concerns your daily life experience, including upholding your vows and commitments—your *samaya*—and ensuring that all your activities are in harmony with the Dharma. If you cultivate the proper view, meditation, and conduct but lack the skills for practice between formal meditation sessions, your commitments will decline. Then hindrances and obstacles will lead to a hell of unrelenting pain. It is essential to diligently monitor your thoughts and behavior with mindfulness and introspection to skillfully determine which actions to adopt and which to reject.

The great master Padmasambhava said:

My view is as high as the sky.
My conduct regarding cause and effect is as fine as barley flour.

Therefore, reject a casual attitude and be meticulous in observing the law of cause and effect. Some practitioners with little experience and understanding become proud and arrogant, which can lead to their downfall. There are many *samaya*s in the vajrayana, but the most important is your *samaya* with the root Guru. Why? Because the Guru is a sacred object. As is said: Accomplishment depends on the vajra master.

See the Guru's body, speech, and mind as the extraordinary enlightened body, speech, and mind of a buddha. Keeping your *samaya* is of utmost importance. Never think of the Guru as an ordinary being. If you do, accomplishment is as far away as the earth from the sun. You may wonder why. It is said that great accomplishment follows the vajra master. The blessings you receive depend upon keeping your *samaya* with the vajra master.

Relying on the vajra master and receiving empowerment and oral instructions, you carefully guard your *samaya* with devotion and loyalty. If you do not maintain the view and meditation diligently, you will not be skillful in the path of conduct that follows, and your vows and *samaya* may decline. There will be obstacles and impediments. Therefore, always be vigilant and attentive, never confusing what must be rejected with what must be adopted. Keep the *samaya* precepts intact, and remain free of faults and setbacks.

The practitioner of Great Perfection cares most for the benefit of others. Care for all sentient beings as much as you care for yourself. Consider their needs and feelings to be of higher importance. Dedicate your life to the well-being of others without a single selfish thought.

All the *samayas* of the secret mantra vehicle are contained within the *samaya* of the Guru. If you see a single fault in the Guru's body, speech, or mind, your blessings and accomplishments could be delayed for months or years. If you disrespect the Guru, speak harshly, or criticize the Guru, you will not receive blessings quickly.

At first, before you receive teachings and instructions from the Guru, you are relying on yourself alone. Once you rely on the Guru and are linked through initiation and instructions, you have no power to break your *samaya*. When you enter this path, you have no choice but to keep *samaya* with the Guru. Keeping *samaya* is not for the Guru's benefit but for your own. Maintaining *samaya* with the Guru means never straying from the continuum of pure awareness.

To keep *samaya* with your Dharma friends, hold in high esteem all those who have entered the door of the Buddha's teachings. In particular, those disciples who share the mandala of the same teacher should view each other as intimate vajra brothers and sisters, with kind hearts and pure perception.

All sentient beings, without exception, have been our kind parents. Alas, they are all burdened by the fear and suffering of samsara. If you do not protect them, then who will? Unable to bear this thought, train your mind by sustaining compassion and accomplish whatever you can through the three doors of body, speech, and mind. Do only what benefits others, and dedicate all your merit to them.

Until your qualities and understanding reach perfection, it is not wise to share your spiritual accomplishments and experiences with others. Do not boast about the hardships you've endured during retreat. Minimize idle behaviors, unnecessary talk, and negative thoughts. Do not try to hide your flaws, nor speak of others' faults. Practice simply and earnestly for the rest of your life. For your main practice, diligently maintain the profound experience of view and meditation. In your day-to-day life, keep to the *samaya* of knowing what to accept and reject. Good qualities will dawn as a matter of course.

Take others with you on your journey, including those who support you and those who mistreat you. Whether good or bad, accept them all with kindness. At all times, be confident and strong. Inwardly keep your spirits high, and outwardly, remain humble. Dress modestly. And avoid clinging to outward appearances.

Fix your ambition on the life of a beggar, content with little. In brief, take your own mind as a witness and pledge your entire life to the Dharma. At the time of death, be free of thoughts about what you have left undone, and feel no shame or regret. When death nears, give away all your possessions and wealth without attachment to any of it. In the best case, at the moment of death, one is filled with joy; in the middling case, one has no fear or apprehension; and in the least, one has no regrets. If the clear light of realization dawns both day and night, there will be no bardo, and death will only amount to the loss of the physical body. Otherwise, if you have confidence that you will be liberated in the intermediate state, whatever you do is fine. If you lack such confidence, but have trained in *phowa*, you can transfer your consciousness to a pure land of your choice and progress along the grounds and paths toward enlightenment.

This revered lineage of ours isn't based only on stories from the past. Even today, yogis who have perfected the practices of *trekchod* (cutting through) and *togal* (direct crossing over) leave this earth dissolving into rainbow light. Many yogis have attained enlightenment in this way. It's miraculous!

Dudjom Rinpoche concludes: "Being fortunate to have found such profound instructions that are the heart blood of the ḍakinis' wisdom, do not throw these precious gems away and go searching for trinkets! Therefore, uplift yourself and meditate with joy! All my devoted disciples, keep this advice as your heart's treasure, and there may be great benefit!"

THE INNER TREASURE OF SELF-LIBERATION

Before we begin this teaching on the inner treasure of self-liberation, having paid homage to my kind root teacher and all the great masters who have transmitted these teachings, it is crucial to generate pure motivation free of selfish agendas, dualistic conceptions, and hopes and fears. We can make this gathering meaningful by understanding how the enlightened masters practiced and achieved realization. The lineage masters' way of living and their realization of the essence of emptiness demonstrate this wonderful and joyous way of being.

The only way to free oneself from suffering is to realize the nature of mind. In other words, only through enlightenment can we experience the ultimate joy and pleasure of being our authentic selves. Since this enlightened essence exists within us, we don't need to seek it from outside.

Some believe they can pay a fee and buy the teachings from the Lama. However, one should never see the teacher as a deer and oneself as the hunter pursuing meat. Thinking this way would only prevent someone from truly benefiting from the Dharma. It would only deepen the ignorance rooted in the conditional egocentric self.

You must see yourself as a patient suffering from desire, attachment, ignorance, jealousy, pride, and so on. Think of the teacher as a doctor, the Dharma as medicine, and the medicine as the cure for the suffering of samsara. With devotion, you should respect and care for the kind teacher, who always acts as a mirror for you. Practicing the Dharma this way will nurture and support you, freeing you from self-centeredness. Only the authentic spiritual teacher can guide you to freedom from selfishness and the afflictions of samsara.

Therefore, first and foremost, we prostrate ourselves to the teacher and the teacher's wisdom lineage. Without my teachers, I would not be on the right path now. I could have been spoiled by fame, fortune, power, and all the world's desirable yet fleeting things.

The mind is inherently clear and pure from the beginning. However, the minds of sentient beings are obscured; thus, we should pray that all beings recognize the true nature of mind and be liberated from the suffering that is caused by ignorance. We empathize with them and realize that we are all in the same state of confusion. In this lifetime, we cultivate compassion and pray for the inner treasure of freedom and self-liberation for ourselves and all sentient beings.

•••

Now, we will review *The Melodious Sound of the Heavenly Drum*, a work by the great master Patrul Ripoche, which my teacher passed down to me.

First, Patrul Rinpoche pays homage to his teacher with three prostrations and then offers prayers: "You who have shown kindness to countless beings with great understanding and patience, I pay homage. You are constantly engaged in compassionate activities for the benefit of others. You are the regent of all enlightened beings. You are the light of compassion. My teacher, I take refuge in you!"

Then, Patrul Rinpoche pays homage to the Dharma: "All the sutras, shastras, and tantras are precious expressions of the truth. With these nectar-like teachings flowing from my teacher's voice to my ears, may I always be sustained by his wisdom. If I can embody the qualities of a serene and peaceful way of being, perhaps some may be pleased to hear about it."

Therefore, Patrul Rinpoche describes the qualities of quiet and secluded retreat locations. He says those who wish to hear it can undertake a meaningful journey and cultivate a compassionate mind. In these places, you won't have to answer to anyone. You are there only to meditate and tame your unruly mind. When you are on your own, there is no one to distract you, inciting attachment and aversion.

The meditation place could be on a remote hillside or in a quiet room in your home. But the true inner retreat is a mind free from hopes and fears, free from discursive thoughts and dualistic confusion, and free from conditioned habits and ego-centered self. In this tranquil space, sitting alone, you cultivate a sense of renunciation. It is like the light of the sun in the sky of non-attachment; the moon's calming glow in the darkness of night.

Patrul Rinpoche says, "Wake up! In the illusory world of samsara, everything appears to exist independently. Due to the seeds of karma and habitual patterns, sentient beings are constantly in motion, engaged in never-ending mundane activities. Our thoughts and feelings, hopes and fears, run continuously, without pause. I cannot see any sign of happiness here; it's like searching for stars in the daytime. So, why wouldn't we feel sad? Why wouldn't we want to renounce this unsatisfactory realm of samsara with full conviction?

Then why wouldn't we be eager to hear the truth of Dharma? Who wouldn't be interested in Dharma, the teachings of the enlightened ones? Especially in these degenerate times, it's so difficult to relate to those who behave like demons, filled with anger, hatred, jealousy, and suspicion. Our friends and partners, those we spend time with, often create more neurosis, more disturbing emotions, and negative feelings. Friends can stir up more desire within us and provoke greater attachment, envy, and pride. How rare it is to find a friend who encourages virtue in us!"

Patrul Rinpoche gives us a metaphor about bees gathering nectar. He says we accumulate wealth like bees collecting nectar to make honey. However, as with the bees, in the end, we do not get to enjoy all that we have gathered. At the time of death, everything we have acquired—fame, fortune, possessions, friends, and relationships—brings nothing but attachment, clinging, and longing, creating a chain that binds us to this world when we must depart. This is the source of grief and sorrow. All that we enjoy feels pleasurable, but ultimately leads to suffering. If we examine this closely, it becomes clear that in samsara there is nothing that brings enduring happiness.

Patrul Rinpoche advises us to care for ourselves and practice the Dharma with a single-minded focus. We genuinely strive to follow this authentic path. Once we pursue the path, the only thing that truly matters is our ability to free ourselves from suffering and help liberate others from suffering.

The more we distract ourselves and get entangled with mundane activities, the more confused and deluded we become. Distractions will only grow. What could be more harmful and deceptive than distraction? It isn't easy to control this monkey mind. When we tame the mind and its habits, we realize the true nature of the mind. Nothing is more magical and precious than understanding the essence of the mind. Patrul Rinpoche says, "In this degenerate time, if you are good at pleasing many people with your charm, it is a clear sign you are distracted by hopes, fears, and ambitions. Conversely, if you cannot please even one person but are living honestly and without deception, you will be pleasing all the buddhas."

•••

This is profound advice from the consummate teacher, Patrul Rinpoche, which I, too, have taken to heart.

Being free from distraction in a quiet dwelling place is the ultimate way to live one's life, and the Buddha praises this as the superior way. Therefore, retreat places and remote meditation sites are the sources of all knowledge and wisdom—the inner treasure of self-realization. If you stay and practice following your teacher's guidance in these places, you will draw closer and closer to liberation.

When liberated from ignorance, you will be protected by all the buddhas and bodhisattvas, who will appear as teachers and bless you with the nectar of luminous wisdom teachings. You will naturally engage in accumulating merit and perform virtuous deeds. There will be no sloth or laziness when you are driven by the intention to be diligent on the path. You will not be pushed off the precipice of attachment, aversion, or ignorance. Your eyes will shed tears of unconditional love, and your heart will overflow with compassion for others and devotion to the teacher.

This is the benefit of meditation in quiet retreat places—the inner treasure of self-liberation. This is the heavenly sound of the melodious drum!

You can find a place for a quiet retreat anywhere. If you live in a city, your shrine room could serve as that retreat. Resolutely, remain there and examine your mind. Tame your unruly thoughts and focus on the value of your human life. Is it more important to frantically chase your thoughts or to reflect on this precious human life? Appreciate this rare and valuable human existence. Only then will you truly value your time and focus on what is essential!

•••

Question: You spoke of the negativity of attaching to wealth and possessions. Can one practice the Dharma and still improve by having some level of wealth for comfort and security?

Rinpoche: Yes, absolutely. With this practice, you'll still be able to meet your needs. You will operate normally, but your priorities will change. You may gain some material wealth, but if your focus is on accumulating wealth, you'll waste your precious life, and at the time of death, you'll feel deep regret.

Question: Can you say more about this idea of self-liberation?

Rinpoche: To liberate ourselves, we must begin with whatever we have in our lives. We have desire, we have anger, we have pride. We have dualistic conceptions and habitual behavior. We can make use of all of this to our advantage. This becomes the fuel that feeds enlightenment. Let's say you experience strong desire. In your meditative practice, you look at the nature of this desire. That very desire will be the key to realizing your true essence. That desire becomes your path to freedom. The energy of desire is nothing other than the expression of your self-liberated nature, the state of emptiness, where there is no birth, cessation, or inherently existing self. All your negative emotions and mental afflictions have no intrinsic existence; they all burst like bubbles in the water.

In your meditation, become familiar with this luminous essence. Then, you can use all of your negativity to liberate yourself on the spot. You need to practice with your desire, hatred, envy, greed, and pride because these poisons will appear in your life. Liberate them all with compassion and insight. This is the inner treasure of self-liberation!

THE ORNAMENT OF GENUINE BEING

The essence of mind, the original ground, is uncontrived and unelaborated. The original ground is beyond accepting or rejecting, beyond holding on or letting go, beyond all dualistic conceptions. There are no mental afflictions or clinging to habitual tendencies on this pure ground. The state of genuine being transcends all limits of past, present, and future. Genuine being is the luminously clear state, where nothing is added and nothing is taken away from its pure original nature. The Omniscient One, Longchenpa said:

Without effort or endeavor, rest in the uncontrived state of genuine being.

A genuine being is free from all selfish agendas. In the state of genuine being, all actions are effortlessly and spontaneously accomplished.

When we cling to our sense of self, our conditioned thoughts seem real to us. For instance, if we hold onto an angry thought, it can persist for days, months, or years. This thought acts like a veil, obscuring the original purity of genuine being—the ultimate ground that is always good.

We are not being authentic when we cling to a false sense of identity. This so-called self has its own conditional motives. For example, if we help a friend, we expect something in return. However, the self we identify with does not exist independently. It is like a mirage—appearing real, but upon further analysis, it is nowhere to be found.

Spiritual practice is not about the current obsession with self-improvement. Being genuine means being true to yourself and embracing who you truly are. You might consider yourself good or bad, but these labels are ultimately meaningless. The essence of the practice is to understand that our thoughts can never truly grasp the depth and wonder of genuine being.

Don't rely too much on your thoughts; instead, trust in your pure, unconditional nature. When you tell a friend, "I love you," it might not be entirely genuine. In moments of selfless non-duality, there is real connection—no separation between self and other. It can't be fully put into words. It is ease and fulfillment, beyond the tension caused by dualistic distinctions.

When practicing meditation, observe the mind's activity. Thoughts will arise and fade away continuously. Be like a neutral observer. Don't chase after the thought or run away from it. Don't accept the thought or reject it. Don't embrace the thought or condemn the thought. Integrate with the flow of energetic awareness without getting entangled in thoughts.

With diligent practice, meditation transforms into a state of non-meditation, where you rest easily, like an old dog basking in the sun. In the vast, sky-like nature of the mind, there is no place for thoughts to linger. Discursive thinking fosters insecurity and lack of confidence in the inconceivable and inexpressible essence of mind itself. When it comes to understanding your true nature, thoughts hold little significance. Conceptual knowledge can never fully reveal the actual meaning or the ultimate truth.

Staying present and aware in the moment is essential. However, if awareness wavers, your tricky ego can exploit this vulnerability. It can be helpful to apply an antidote when emotional turmoil suddenly strikes. For instance, patience is an antidote to anger. With forbearance and self-control, you will avoid responding aggressively.

When you release the need to protect or defend your sense of self, you feel a deep sense of openness and freedom. You no longer feel disconnected from others. By shedding the armor of ego, you have nothing to hide. You openly engage with others and accept them as they are. Your expressions become ornaments of genuine being.

You can criticize your friends, make enemies, and cut them out of your life. This is a mistake if you judge them too harshly. If you despise what your friend did yesterday, you're holding onto the past. Respect everyone, and understand that their true nature is inherently good, even when they misbehave or cause harm.

The true nature of genuine being is beyond words. Absolute truth cannot be fathomed by the intellect alone. You may use intellect as a guide, but to embark on this journey, you need the guidance of a qualified and realized teacher. Only then can you experience the ultimate freedom of genuine being!

H.E. Shyalpa Tenzin Rinpoche

PART THREE
KEY TOPICS

TAKING REFUGE IN THE THREE JEWELS

When you take refuge in the Three Jewels, you open the outer door to the Buddha, Dharma, and Sangha. You unlock the inner door to the Lama, Yidam, and Dakini, and the secret door to the Dharmakaya, Sambhogakaya, and Nirmanakaya. You realize that there is no reliable refuge elsewhere. Relying on good health, relationships, steady work, and material possessions are all conditional and impermanent; they will eventually betray you.

When you take refuge, you call upon the unconditional strength and wisdom of the awakened ones, as well as the guidance and support of a community of realized teachers. Fearing the sufferings of samsara, you seek the protection of an authentic and infallible refuge. You aspire to be an honorable being—a compassionate friend to all humanity.

With no time to waste, you don't indulge in wishful thinking. It's your good fortune to have a precious human life that allows you to hear and assimilate the teachings of the enlightened Buddha.

Don't invest too much time and energy in mundane worldly affairs; have just enough to live well. The best investment you can make is in the Three Jewels—the spiritual richness and wealth of the Buddha, Dharma, and Sangha.

LIGHTING A BUTTER LAMP

The butter lamp symbolizes the light that drives away the darkness of ignorance. You light the lamp and pray for the flame to shine in everyone's heart.

You can imagine the butter lamp as expansive as the universe, and the butter as abundant as the water in a vast ocean. Then picture offering the light to the buddhas and bodhisattvas, and to all sentient beings. This is a wonderful way to create merit and purify karma.

You can make a butter lamp using butter and a wick. In Tibet, it is customary to light a butter lamp at home or in temples. Even the poorest families who have little food to eat choose to light a butter lamp as a daily practice. Make a butter lamp or use an ordinary candle to ignite the flame of wisdom, and pray for the welfare of all sentient beings!

VALUE YOUR TIME

Today, many people say their lives are too busy, leaving little time for spiritual practice. But this might just be an excuse. If you're feeling overwhelmed, it's important to simplify. Create more space to relax and enjoy your life through moments of deep relaxation and quiet reflection.

I don't feel the need to surround myself with material possessions. Above all, I value freedom—freedom from all selfish desires and attachments. This is what truly matters. I am not interested in accumulating wealth, nor do I feel the need to acquire anything for myself. These are lessons I learned from my enlightened teachers.

If there is anything truly valuable in life, it is being fully immersed in the richness of this present moment. We always have this moment, and it should be free from the burdens of the past and worries about the future. When we regret the past or anticipate the future, the freedom inherent in this present moment is lost.

We must take care of ourselves, our family, and our friends. This is our daily responsibility, and it is manageable. What is difficult is managing our desires. The more desires we have, the more distractions we create, and the less time we have to enjoy our freedom.

If we desire more and more, it soon becomes unmanageable. There is no end to desires. We should understand how desire begins and how it can be addressed. If you can manage your desires, that's a good start. You will have more than enough time to help yourself and benefit others.

THE KINDNESS OF THE TEACHER

Glorious root teacher, precious one,
Dwelling on a lotus seat on the crown of my head,
Hold me with your great kindness.
Bestow the accomplishment of body, speech, and mind.

How do students connect with and relate to the teacher? This topic, particularly within the vajrayana tradition, is essential and often taken too lightly. The relationship between student and teacher should be very pure, not rooted in personal gain, ambition, or power.

Students are at fault when they fail to follow the teacher's instructions. The teacher must explain to the students how to conduct themselves properly. The teacher should never be disrespected, looked down upon, or belittled. Whether you agree or disagree with your teachers, show them your respect and always remember their kindness.

In the vajrayana, your practice depends on the authenticity of your relationship with your teacher. The teacher's role is to guide and instruct disciples, always speaking the truth, whether or not they choose to accept it. While I may not see myself as an exceptional teacher, I strive to be honest and straightforward with my students and not compromise. If students behave poorly, it can harm them, and I must point this out; otherwise, I would be cheating them.

Genuine teachers are fully committed to their students' growth. They share their knowledge and guidance selflessly, expecting nothing in return. Their only hope is for their students to practice sincerely and mature on the path of Dharma. True teachers do not seek recognition, praise, or honors for themselves.

First and foremost, students must recognize the teacher's immeasurable compassion and kindness. Without a teacher, navigating pitfalls on the spiritual path is nearly impossible. Like a mirror, the teacher reflects the intelligence of one's own nature. Always keep the teacher in your heart and never forget their kindness!

WHO ARE YOU?

Who are you? Do your hopes and fears control you? Is the so-called ego dragging you back into dissatisfaction and grief? To ease the pain, firmly, with conviction, cut the root of all your suffering. Who is it that seeks acknowledgment and recognition? Explore this: look deeply within your heart and mind. After deep reflection, you may realize that the so-called ego does not truly exist.

It is our responsibility to always engage in genuine, compassionate communication. This can only occur when we resist the urge to fabricate and pursue thoughts that mislead us—thoughts driven by selfish desires that repeatedly lead us into confusion. We need to understand who is pursuing these thoughts and where they come from. Who is it that declares, "This is what I like, and this is what I don't like?" What fuels all this hope and fear, expectations and disappointments?

Not knowing who we truly are is the cause of our troubles. It is essential to understand that who we think we are arises and passes every moment. If we cannot rest in the mind of pristine awareness, we'll be constantly caught up in our thoughts and distractions. We will waste our time and energy fighting with our delusions.

BEYOND DEATH

In this life, we are all like temporary travelers. Our lodging is what we call "this body." At some unknown time, the lord of death will appear at our door and tell us that it's time to depart. For many, death can be a traumatic experience. We cling to our bodies, strongly identifying with our physical form. If we are not prepared for this transformation, it can be a frightening and painful experience.

The realized spiritual masters of our lineage were continually mindful of death. They viewed their practice as preparation for dying. Death was seen as the perfect time to celebrate, to release this life and this body, and to die fearlessly, without any regrets.

To live this life fully, we must confront and explore the nature of death. No matter how much we achieve in the material world, we find no lasting fulfillment. When we grow old, frail, and tired, it is too late to prepare ourselves, and we are not prepared to die.

Only in our human form can we, with clear intelligence, liberate ourselves from the darkness of ignorance. Caring for ourselves and making the most of our time is essential. If we do not care for ourselves in this life, we are not using our precious time wisely. In the face of death, we are all vulnerable; no one is immune. Constantly remember the nature of impermanence and the certainty of death.

Retreating to nature and practicing in solitude can be beneficial. The changing colors of the seasons and sudden shifts in weather remind us of the impermanence and fleeting nature of all things. Simplifying your life and learning to thrive with very little can be invigorating, revealing the inherent wealth and richness that exists within you.

We have meaningful lives when we cultivate compassion and unconditional love for ourselves and all sentient beings. We awaken to our luminous nature—timeless, indestructible, and beyond the reach of death and decay.

•••

Question: I have a close friend who is dying of cancer, and it is very upsetting. How can I help him?

Rinpoche: If possible, try to fully embrace your friend with equanimity. In the ultimate sense, there's no need to see him as someone dying of cancer. You will also face death. You will be tormented if you don't understand the nature of life and death, and he will suffer too. We need to accept our vulnerability and the inevitability of death.

Only then can you be honest with yourself and your friend. Clinging to this life is the root of all suffering. Can anyone truly hold on to this conditional life? I don't think so. Promise that you will not deceive yourself or your friend about the reality of death. Then, there is the possibility that you and your friend can celebrate both life and death together with the same acceptance.

LUMINOUS MIND OF COMPASSION

Beginning today, let us cultivate pure motivation and awaken our true nature—the luminous mind of compassion. Lacking compassion, we are destitute. With a compassionate mind, we have all that we need. A compassionate mind is limitless and all-encompassing.

We are fortunate to have this precious human life. This very moment is all there truly is, and it is priceless. From this point forward, let us share this life, this moment, with a loving and compassionate heart.

As you enjoy your meal, take a moment to reflect on all the sentient beings who are desperate and have nothing to eat. Imagine these beings savoring your meal and feeling fulfilled. With a open heart, offer this meal to all who are suffering. In this way, you can nurture your generosity and compassion in every moment of your life.

The luminous mind of compassion is devoid of darkness and radiates light. A mind free from attachment, aversion, and ignorance, this is the essence of our true nature. With a luminous mind of compassion, may we live this life to the fullest.

FOLLOW THE PATH OF TRUE DHARMA

You can always practice the Dharma and live meaningfully, regardless of circumstances. When your conviction is firm, you can overcome every obstacle. If you have this understanding, it brings joy: "I can handle this; I can face this." You feel prepared to tackle every challenge.

Two forces act on us simultaneously. One force draws us into samsara's conditional, indulgent pleasures, while the other uplifts and propels us toward the joy and freedom of spiritual awakening. If you can skillfully direct your energy toward the path of liberation, the fleeting pleasures of the material world will not seduce you. Like a fearless warrior, you will subjugate all negative thoughts and emotions that lack compassion and luminous clarity.

When the great yogi Milarepa entered a mountain cave to meditate, he had only one robe and a small bowl. But he was armored with unwavering trust and confidence in his infallible teacher, Lord Marpa. With steadfast conviction, Milarepa confronted every challenge with the power of unconditional awareness. We can follow Milarepa's example and find freedom from suffering in this very lifetime!

RESTING IN RIGPA

Rigpa is a Tibetan word that means "seeing." What are we seeing, and why is this seeing so important? In Dzogchen, it is understood that our true self-nature is primordially pure and perfect. From this primordially perfect state, everything arises as pure energy, and everything that occurs is an expression of our true self-nature.

Our true self-nature is unconditioned; therefore, it is free from birth and cessation and lacks inherent existence. Mind itself, the essence itself, is emptiness. Its nature is clarity, and its expression is appearance inseparable from emptiness.

Here, when we say "emptiness inseparable from appearance," we mean that whatever appears does not have a truly existing self-nature. However, when we fail to see this, all appearances seem to exist as concrete entities. As a result, we become tormented and stuck in the endless cycle of samsara.

When we are in the unconditional state of *rigpa*, there is no experiencer separate from the experience. There is no "you" apart from the experience itself; it is complete. This completeness is beyond the reach of words or characterization. This completeness is the magic. When there is *rigpa*, seeing is crystal-clear. There are no concepts—no "this is how it should be or shouldn't be." There is no hesitation, no strategizing, and no wavering. There is no trace of "I." Self-confidence arises naturally; it is not manufactured

Rigpa is the indestructible wish-fulfilling jewel. Within the unconditional state of pure awareness, everything is included.

What is the difference between enlightened beings and sentient beings? The former recognizes *rigpa*, while the latter, obscured by ignorance, does not see it. Enlightened beings breathe pure air; sentient beings breathe karmic air. However, both have buddha nature. Sentient beings fail to recognize their true self-nature.

You do not need to be a great philosopher or a learned scholar to recognize *rigpa* and realize Dzogchen. An unschooled cowherd can realize *rigpa* as quickly as the most learned scholar. In an instant, when the teacher points out *rigpa*, you either realize it or you don't. If you see it, you have received the most extraordinary wish-fulfilling jewel. Patrul Rinpoche said, "When you have *rigpa*, nothing more is needed. Maintaining *rigpa* then becomes the only essential practice. Everything appears the same when I see the nature of all phenomena; therefore, what more is there to understand? Even if I do not pursue many studies, I am happy because I embody this *rigpa*!"

If you attain the ultimate realization of *rigpa*, you should not abandon your other practices. With *rigpa*, you will become the most disciplined and responsible being. You will not be crude, flamboyant, or careless. You will be precise in your speech and skillful in your actions because *rigpa* is the authentic expression of enlightened awareness. You will see and experience the beauty of Dzogchen.

UNBORN AWARENESS

We believe our thoughts accurately reflect conditional reality. Thoughts shift and change from moment to moment, yet we fail to recognize that each thought is like a mirage. One thought after another deceives us, just appearing to be true. A rainbow seems to exist, but you can't grasp a rainbow. Thoughts are like rainbows; you can't find their source or origin. In such moments, you transcend thought and go beyond past, present, and future.

What remains when your mind is no longer caught in the past, present, and future? There is awareness. You can call it whatever you wish, but in the Dzogchen tradition, we call it pure awareness. This awareness is not born; it has no beginning; therefore, it has no end. Thoughts condition the energy of mind; awareness is pure and unconditioned. Awareness is not a thing; it cannot be identified. Awareness is without root or foundation. Thus, in awareness, there is no "I" and no "other." The "I" and the "other" are born from conditioned thought.

Our ultimate essence is unborn and unceasing awareness. *Rigpa* is another term for being one with your true nature. In the continuum of unborn awareness, the "I" as such does not exist. In Dzogchen, we say there is nothing to meditate on; this is the Dzogchen style of non-meditation.

When practicing Dzogchen, we have glimpses of *rigpa*—unborn awareness. However, glimpses alone are not enough. Until the state of unborn awareness is fully stabilized, we must be diligent in our practice; otherwise, we risk becoming tormented again by our ordinary, mundane thoughts. Please continue to practice with confidence and trust in unborn awareness, the true nature of mind itself!

RELATIVE AND ABSOLUTE

How do we reveal and actualize our buddha nature—our enlightened essence? There are two ways: the relative and the absolute.

In the relative way, we cultivate compassion and kindness with pure motivation. We recognize others' suffering by acknowledging our own struggles and pain. We become aware of our own vulnerabilities and those of others. We give generously to those in need. We discipline our conduct and take sublime vows. We cultivate forbearance by practicing patience. We diligently accumulate merit by living mindfully. We meditate to still and calm the mind so that we can see things more clearly.

The ultimate approach is to perceive everything we do, see, think, and feel—whether good or bad—as if it were the magic of a master magician. A skilled magician can make us perceive what is not real—something that doesn't exist. In this life, everything that appears resembles the work of a master magician. Birth is like that, and death is like that. Pleasure is like that, and pain is like that. Good is like that; bad is like that. By understanding in this way, you will be able to remain at ease. You will come to recognize the absolute nature of mind beyond philosophical opinions, beyond concepts or language, which is emptiness. In Dzogchen, we call this the primordial purity of mind itself.

Relative and absolute are inseparable. When you unite these two, your practice is complete. You cannot dismiss the conventional laws of relative truth, nor can you ignore the absolute wisdom of mind without suffering the consequences. Doing so would be an extreme nihilistic view, leading to self-destruction. It is essential to uphold the relative practice of kindness and compassion while remaining grounded in the absolute wisdom of the unconditional mind itself.

This is the key. When relative and absolute are inseparable, all things become clear, and everything awakens you.

THE SEVEN LINE PRAYER

HUNG!
On the Northwest border of the country of Uddiyana,
On the anthers of a lotus flower,
You attained the marvelous supreme siddhi.
Renowned as the Lotus Born,
Surrounded by a retinue of many dakinis,
Following in your footsteps, I will practice.
Please come and grant your blessings!
GURU PEMA SIDDHI HUNG

Traditionally, the Seven Line Prayer is recited three times at the beginning of sadhana practice in Dzogchen.

What does the prayer mean, and why is it recited three times? When you recite the prayer the first time, visualize Padmasambhava at the crown of your head, and the visualization becomes clear. This visualization is a conceptual creation of your mind that, in itself, does not possess the full power to bless you.

The second time you recite the prayer, you invoke the wisdom of Padmasambhava and summon his blessings.

Padmasambhava embodies the essence of enlightened mind; therefore, visualizing Guru Padmasambhava awakens your own enlightened qualities.

The third time you recite, you feel the Guru's absolute strength and power, and you supplicate Padmasambhava for his blessings, guidance, and protection.

In Dzogchen practice, when you recite with vivid faith and devotion, *visualization, invocation, and supplication* can happen spontaneously and all at once. For the Dzogchen practitioner, the Seven Line Prayer is a profound and powerful practice that invokes blessings, purifies obscurations, and gathers merit and wisdom.

Guru Padmasambhava shared this wisdom with Lady Yeshe Tsogyal: Reciting the Vajra Guru mantra will bring inconceivable benefits and power. One will be protected from plague, famine, warfare, and bad omens. The Vajra Guru mantra is the heart essence of all deities.

OM... is the supreme essence of enlightened body
AH... is the supreme essence of enlightened speech
HUNG... is the supreme essence of enlightened mind
Vajra... is the essence of the vajra family
Guru... is the essence of the ratna family
Padma... is the essence of the padma family
Siddhi... is the essence of the karma family
Hung .... is the essence of the buddha family

This is for a general understanding. According to the heart essence of Dzogchen teaching, the mantra can be explained in twelve different ways.

OM AH HUNG VAJRA GURU PADMA SIDDHI HUNG

VAJRA PRIDE

Vajra pride is pure and indestructible energy. It is free and independent, never captured by or dependent on ego. Vajra pride does not cling to an ego-centered self. When the light of vajra pride shines, there is no darkness. The dignity of vajra pride embodies diamond-like compassion for all suffering beings. Witnessing the depth of this suffering and feeling it profoundly, one sheds tears of heartrending compassion. Vajra pride is intimately connected to all beings and helps to liberate them from the suffering of attachment, aversion, and ignorance.

Vajra pride is like a tree with roots planted in the rich soil of humility. It is neither arrogant nor coarse. It adapts to whatever is needed. Vajra pride resembles a wise old grandfather who enjoys relaxing and playing with his grandchildren. Grandpa helps the kids build a sandcastle on the beach and invites the prince and princess into their beautiful castle. Grandpa knows the castle is an illusion, but he is happy to play along. Later, when the waves wash it away, Grandpa reassures his grandchildren, saying, "Don't cry; we'll build another castle tomorrow."

Vajra Pride is the wisdom that expresses goodwill for all of humanity.

CONQUERING SELF-DECEPTION

Eventually, we will all face sickness, aging, and death. There is no way to avoid the decline of our health and strength. No matter how powerful we are or how much control we have over our environment, we cannot control the length of our lives or the timing of our death. Regardless of how clever or intelligent we are, we deceive ourselves if we ignore the natural outcome of our human existence.

You can continue to deceive yourself until reality strikes. At that moment, your mind may not be agile enough to face the truth, leaving you feeling hopeless. Now, the wise choice is to avoid self-deception and sincerely strive to see things as they are. By following the spiritual path, you gain the courage to realize the ultimate freedom of awakening to the profound essence of Dzogchen, the Great Perfection, enabling you to embrace your life fully and completely. So, isn't it sensible to be truly honest with yourself and live openly now in the freshness of this moment?

THE ULTIMATE PATH

All of the Bodhisattva's attainments, including the wisdom and compassion found in countless teachings, are distilled into great compassion, which is inseparable from emptiness. We often call compassion the "king of the heart," referring to emptiness endowed with great compassion.

The glorious Mahasiddha Saraha expressed in his songs of realization that those who speak of emptiness but lack great compassion are not on the supreme path and will remain mired in samsara. However, those who realize the inseparability of emptiness and great compassion hold the jewel of enlightenment in the palm of their hand. Furthermore, the Great Nagarjuna stated that the essence of everything—emptiness inseparable from great compassion—is the only way to understand the true nature of mind.

Great compassion, inseparable from emptiness, is the only remedy capable of healing the mental afflictions of attachment, hatred, pride, ignorance, false views, and doubt. Many practitioners claim to understand emptiness, but they may be merely boasting. It is essential to realize emptiness, inseparable from profound compassion. This is the ultimate path.

The essence of Dharma is emptiness, inseparable from great compassion. How is all of Dharma encompassed in this understanding? If you realize the truth of emptiness, inseparable from great compassion, you will experience little desire, grasping, or clinging. You will see no distinction between yourself and others, no difference between what is yours and what is theirs. This mind is free from hostility and hatred and imbued with peace and kindness.

The great master Atisha was once asked, "Is realizing emptiness, inseparable from great compassion, the only way to attain complete enlightenment?" The master affirmed this, saying, "Yes, everything that one sees, hears, and thinks is nothing but the creation of one's mind." This reflects the view of the inseparable nature of emptiness and compassion: All that appears has no inherent existence. Familiarizing oneself with this view is the essence of meditation. Those who embrace this view accumulate merit for themselves and others, attaining great blessings. The Buddha provided all 84,000 teachings of Dharma to guide all sentient beings toward this ultimate truth.

APPENDIX

SPONTANEOUS VERSE ON PRECIOUS HUMAN LIFE

By Shyalpa Tenzin Rinpoche

Seeing the preciousness of human life is such a great joy!
Realize this preciousness.
Seeing the preciousness of life,
Energy flows unobstructed, like a river surging toward
  the ocean.

When we lack respect for ourselves,
Engulfed in negativity,
We fail to appreciate this precious human life.
There is nothing sadder than this.

When you find yourself on an island of gold
Don't go home empty-handed.
Here and now, pick up the gold,
And see the preciousness of that!

Crying inside is true crying.
Tears flow when you see how time is wasted,
Not aware of how precious life is.

Now you realize:
How fortunate. How wonderful!
You celebrate with tears!
Weeping comes from the inside out.
Tears flow when you see the preciousness of life.
You touch a nerve inside: the spark of a precious
human life.

Seeing the infallible nature of the teacher,
You see potential in everyone.
There is great respect for all sentient beings.

You have devotion to the teacher
Who is like a snow mountain.
The sun of devotion shines on the mountain,
And the nectar flows.
The sun of devotion melts the snow
And you drink the nectar!
You taste the juice that is your life!
A juicy life, not a dry life.
When the sun shines, the juice comes.
When you open yourself, the juice comes.

Autumn leaves fall from the trees.
You are free to be yourself;
You watch the leaves scatter.
At that time, there is enrichment.
You respect yourself.
That brings dignity.
That brings confidence.
That frees you from fantasizing—
a mind that just spins around.
You don't chase after every thought.

Completely at ease,
You cannot be misled.
You cannot be shaken.
This would not be difficult for you.
It just comes naturally.

It's funny! Like a dream!
Today we are here; tomorrow we are gone.
Life will have no meaning,
Unless we see the preciousness of human life.
Ordinary achievements in this life mean nothing at all,
Unless we see the preciousness.
Chasing worldly things is like chasing a mirage,
Grasping them, they burst like bubbles,
Seen in a dream.

Don't believe that life has a destination.
If you're going somewhere,
You miss so much.
You lose so much.
Remember, this moment is complete.

When you get somewhere,
You get nowhere.
When you are nowhere,
You embrace life.
You relish this life!

On this journey of life,
Be like a skilled dancer.
Fully engaged in the dancing,
The dance is your journey,
And your journey is the dance.

Don't consider yourself first.
Always heed the circumstances.
Be flexible and follow the tune.
The circumstance is the music,
And you become the dancer.
Dance with joy and flair!

Dancers are never too young.
Dancers are never too old.
It's never too late to dance.
Dance with grace and compassion.
With compassion as your partner,
You will dance well on any stage.
Anytime. Anywhere.

With flexibility,
You will not rule anything out,
Or rule anything in.
You will be ready for the unpredictable
In a predictable human life.

As a follower of Dharma,
Don't be a slouch.
Don't be rigid.
Don't be predictable.

Remain freely, in simplicity and kindness.
This will benefit you,
And benefit all sentient beings!

THE FINAL TESTAMENT OF PADAMPA SANGYE

At a Dzogchen retreat, Shyalpa Tenzin Rinpoche gave an oral translation from the Tibetan text.

When the great Acharya, Padampa Sangye, was ill and nearing death, his disciple, Charchenpa, came to see him. Charchenpa wept and said, "On whom shall we, the people of Tingri, rely? Then, he gave his final instructions to the townspeople of Tingri, "The Final Testament of Padampa Sangye."

Practice the sacred Dharma with body, speech, and mind;
People of Tingri, there is nothing finer than this.

Wholeheartedly rely on the Three Jewels;
People of Tingri, blessings will come swiftly.

Give up the aims of this worldy life, practice for lives to come;
People of Tingri, this is the supreme practice.

Families are ephemeral, like crowds in the market;
People of Tingri, don't quarrel and fight.

Wealth and possessions are like a magic show;
People of Tingri, don't be bound by knots of greed.

This body is a bag of unclean substances;
People of Tingri, don't pamper or indulge it.

Family and friends are the play of illusion;
People of Tingri, don't let affection tie you up.

Your land is like a nomad's temporary dwelling;
People of Tingri, cut your craving and attachment.

The six realms of beings are shared by all;
People of Tingri, don't think of them as "I" or "mine."

The moment of birth is the first sign of death;
People of Tingri, there is no time to waste.

Without distraction, practice the precious Dharma;
People of Tingri, it will guide you at the time of death.

The consequences of cause and effect will surely ripen;
People of Tingri, avoid all negative actions.

Actions are like things seen in a dream;
People of Tingri, practice nonaction.

When you get what you want, it does not last;
People of Tingri, you have everything you need.

As you can't remain in this world for long;
People of Tingri, prepare for your journey now.

In the forest, monkeys frolic and play;
People of Tingri, but the forest is engulfed by fire.

Birth, aging, sickness, and death are a river of suffering;
People of Tingri, prepare your boat to cross over.

On the narrow pathway of birth, death, and intermediate state,
The bandits of the five poisons await to attack;
People of Tingri, summon the teacher for an escort.

With the embrace of the teacher, you will never fall down;
People of Tingri, always carry the teacher on the crown of
your head.

With the protection of the teacher, you can go wherever
you wish;
People of Tingri, offer your devotion as fare for the journey.

Where there is wealth, there is avarice;
People of Tingri, give generously to all.

Where there is power, there is wrongdoing;
People of Tingri, give up your desire for power.

Grasping for wealth and power brings no pleasure;
People of Tingri, give up desire for gain.

You leave this life without friends or relations;
People of Tingri, rely only on Dharma.

The day you die, no one can help you;
People of Tingri, rely on yourself.

If you remember your death, you want nothing in this life;
People of Tingri, remember your death.

Like shadows of the setting sun, death draws nearer to you;
People of Tingri, prepare now for your escape.

A flower in the morning withers in the evening;
People of Tingri, don't trust in this body.

When alive, you treat your body like a god,
After death, it is a frightening demon;
People of Tingri, don't be deceived by this illusory body.

People meet on market day and then they disperse
and disappear;
People of Tingri, your friends will surely depart.

Illusory appearances have no essence;
People of Tingri, create auspicious conditions for practice.

Soon, the vulture of this mind will pass away;
People of Tingri, soar up into the sky.

All sentient beings of the six realms have been your
kind parents;
People of Tingri, look upon them with kindness
and compassion.

Hatred for enemies brings negative karma;
People of Tingri, abandon your hatred.

Prostration and circumambulation purify negative actions;
People of Tingri, abandon useless activities.

Mantras and prayers purify harmful speech;
People of Tingri, avoid meaningless gossip.

Fervent devotion purifies habitual thoughts;
People of Tingri, always remember the teacher.

In the end, you leave flesh and bones behind;
People of Tingri, don't think that your life is permanent.

The ultimate refuge is the unchanging natural state of mind;
People of Tingri, rely only on that.

The most precious wealth is the treasure of mind itself;
People of Tingri, this treasure is never exhausted.

The tastiest food of all is the food of meditation;
People of Tingri, you will never go hungry.

The most delicious drink of all is the nectar of mindfulness,
People of Tingri, the flow of nectar is endless.

The best friend of all is self-arising unborn wisdom;
People of Tingri, from which you are never parted.

The best child is the young child of pure awareness;
People of Tingri, awareness is beyond birth and death.

In the continuum of emptiness, wield the spear of
pure awareness;
People of Tingri, it is beyond defeat and destruction.

The best meditation is undistracted non-meditation;
People of Tingri, it is beyond lethargy and excitation.

In the continuum, remain in the vitality of unobstructed energy;
People of Tingri, conduct does not accept or reject.

Within the self-arising expanse, train in this unceasing energy;
People of Tingri, there is nothing to hope for or fear.

Seek the indivisible four kayas within your own mind;
People of Tingri, without doubt or expectation.

The root of samsara and nirvana is ignorant mind;
People of Tingri, the mind itself has no actual existence.

Delusions are like the flight of a bird in the sky; they leave no trace.
People of Tingri, don't cling to appearances.

The ultimate truth is like the light of the sun;
People of Tingri, the light never wavers.

Thoughts are like thieves in an empty house;
People of Tingri, there is no gain or loss.

Feelings leave no trace, like drawings on water;
People of Tingri, don't cling to illusory appearances.

Thoughts of love and hate are like rainbows in the sky;
People of Tingri, there is nothing to grasp.

The movements of thought are like clouds in the sky;
People of Tingri, in mind itself, there are no points of reference.

Without grasping, thoughts release by themselves;
People of Tingri, like the wind that does not cling.

Pure awareness is like a rainbow in the sky;
People of Tingri, it is unobstructed.

Realization is like a mute person's dream;
People of Tingri, there are no words to express it.

Realization is like the pleasure and joy of youth;
People of Tingri, the bliss cannot be described.

Appearance and emptiness are inseparable;
People of Tingri, like the sky, without a center or boundary.

Mind without distractions is like the mirror;
People of Tingri, it is free of philosophical assertions.

Awareness-emptiness is like reflections in a mirror;
People of Tingri, in the mirror, nothing is born, and
nothing ceases.

Bliss-emptiness is like sunlight on the snow;
People of Tingri, it can't be identified or apprehended.

Talk vanishes without a trace, like an echo;
People of Tingri, sounds are ungraspable.

Happiness and suffering arise like music from the strings of
a lute;
People of Tingri, the sound depends on causes
and conditions.

Views of the world come from within;
People of Tingri, melt the ice of concepts, and water
flows freely.

The working of ignorance is like the gushing of a spring;
People of Tingri, don't try to plug it up.

The delusions of samsara and nirvana are the enemy;
People of Tingri, cultivate virtue as your ally.

The clarity of the five kayas is like a land of gold;
People of Tingri, in a land of gold, have no hope or fear.

This precious human life is like an island of treasure;
People of Tingri, do not leave empty-handed.

The great vehicle of the mahayana is like a wish-fulfilling jewel;
People of Tingri, it is rare and hard to find again.

Have just what you need for food, clothes, and shelter;
People of Tingri, focus on practicing Dharma.

Practice with rigorous training when you are young;
People of Tingri, it gets harder when you're old.

When delusions arise, apply the right antidote;
People of Tingri, delusions will be liberated.

Think often of the sufferings of samsara;
People of Tingri, that will strengthen your faith and devotion.

Right now, be diligent and stand firm;
People of Tingri, be prepared at the time of death.

Like dewdrops in the sun, this life is short and uncertain;
People of Tingri, abandon laziness and sloth.

The Buddha's teachings are like the sun through a break in
the clouds;
People of Tingri, see the light right now.

You give advice but don't apply it to yourself;
People of Tingri, focus on your own faults.

Due to circumstances, pure faith can quickly wane;
People of Tingri, contemplate the faults of samsara.

Negativity can be contagious;
People of Tingri, shun the company of negative friends.

Having virtuous friends, your good qualities grow;
People of Tingri, follow spiritual teachers.

Lies and deceit bring harm to yourself and others;
People of Tingri, let your conscience be your witness.

To lack awareness of your true nature is the root of disaster;
People of Tingri, be mindful and introspective.

If you don't persevere, you cannot claim ultimate victory;
People of Tingri, wear the armor of perseverance.

Like old friends, habitual patterns keep returning;
People of Tingri, relinquish the past.

If your realization is weak, pray to your teacher;
People of Tingri, profound samadhi will arise from within.

Gathering together ends in drifting apart;
People of Tingri, don't be attached to a gathering.

If you aspire to be happy, endure hardship now;
People of Tingri, Buddha will be by your side.

I, the Acharya Padampa Sangye, will not be here long.
I have practiced diligently without distraction;
You, people of Tingri, follow in my footsteps!

A SHORT BIOGRAPHY OF SHYALPA TENZIN RINPOCHE

His Eminence Shyalpa Tenzin Rinpoche was born in the foothills of the Himalayas. His parents were village leaders in Tibet, but after going into exile, they worked in the sun from dawn, felling trees and clearing land for corn harvesting. During this time of hardship, Rinpoche's grandparents served as his primary caregivers, and there were early signs of the course Rinpoche's life would take.

At age two, he placed his hands together in reverence upon entering the local temple. A Buddhist Lama told his grandmother he was destined to become a spiritual leader. When he was four years old, he joined his father at sunrise while performing his rituals and prayers. This marked Rinpoche's first introduction to the sacred practices of Tibetan Buddhism. At age six, he attended public school for a secular education, and after returning home, he read and memorized Buddhist texts until dinnertime. His grandmother kindly encouraged him to work diligently on his spiritual studies.

On his fifteenth birthday, Rinpoche decided to continue his education and gained acceptance at the Central Institute of Higher Tibetan Studies in Sarnath, India. He joined his classmates each morning to study Buddhist philosophy and the science of mind. In the afternoons, he participated in lively philosophical debates. With each passing year, his confidence in the power and authenticity of the Buddha's teachings grew deeper. After nearly seven years of study at the institute, Rinpoche met his root teacher, Kyabje Chatral Rinpoche, Sangye Dorje, near the Ganges River, and studied with him and more than twenty great masters, from whom he received essential instructions, transmissions, and empowerments.

At age twenty-one, Rinpoche was summoned to Riwoche Monastery in Kham, Eastern Tibet, to be installed as the recognized reincarnation of the spiritual leader of Shyalpa Monastery. During his enthronement, the esteemed Lama, Khenpo Karma Dorje, along with other Lamas, performed the Innermost Secret Essence Puja of Padmasambhava. This ritual ceremony pays homage to the Second Buddha, Padmasambhava, who introduced the precious teachings of Buddhism from India to Tibet. Rinpoche felt deeply honored by their warm welcome, and their faith in him strengthened his resolve to take on the responsibility of guiding the monastery.

In 1987, Rinpoche was invited to teach the Dharma in the United States. He was intrigued by the idea, as he had met American tourists in India who told him their country was materially wealthy but spiritually impoverished. Upon arriving in Boston with only a hundred dollars, he embarked on a road trip to Los Angeles and back to the East Coast, offering teachings along the way. Rinpoche was pleased to see the genuine interest of Americans in learning and practicing the Dharma.

His Eminence eventually settled in the Berkshires of Western Massachusetts, where a community of devoted followers and students began to grow. When Rinpoche wasn't giving public teachings, he remained in semi-retreat, meditating on the *Seven Treasuries*, the seminal work of Longchenpa, the preeminent master and scholar of the Nyingma school of Tibetan Buddhism. Rinpoche's appreciation for Longchenpa's teachings deepened, and he wished to share this illuminating wisdom with receptive seekers in the West.

In 1989, Rinpoche founded Rangrig Yeshe, a nonprofit organization to support his teachings and charitable activities in the United States. Later, he received numerous requests for guidance and humanitarian aid from the Himalayas, and in 1992, he established the Shyalpa Monastery and Nunnery in Kathmandu, Nepal. Today, over 100 monks attend Marpa School at the monastery. In the Mipham Shedra, 50 senior monks study advanced Buddhist philosophy and tantric ritual. A learned scholar and adept meditator, Rinpoche has published five books, including The Path to Perfect Freedom.

With the support of followers and Rangrig Yeshe in the United States, His Eminence purchased 50 acres of beautiful land in Millerton, New York, to establish "Buddhafield, The Center for Enlightenment" as his official seat in North America. In 2009, Rinpoche founded the Wencheng Gongzhu International Foundation in Hong Kong, with branches in Taiwan and Malaysia, to facilitate and support his charitable activities across Asia.

In 2013, the Nepalese government entrusted His Eminence with developing a treasured piece of land in Lumbini, Nepal, the birthplace of the Buddha. Rinpoche's vision is to create the ultimate peace destination that honors the sacred birthplace of Prince Siddhartha and serves as a pilgrimage site for visitors of all races, colors, and creeds—a source of universal peace and understanding. The Universal Peace Sanctuary is currently under construction near the Sacred Garden in Lumbini.

THE UNIVERSAL PEACE SANCTUARY & THE UNIVERSAL PEACE FORUM

The Universal Peace Sanctuary

For many years, His Eminence Shyalpa Tenzin Rinpoche envisioned creating a sacred sanctuary for all sentient beings, regardless of race, color, or creed, including both believers and non-believers. The most tranquil place on Earth, the UNESCO World Heritage site in Lumbini, Nepal, was chosen to bring this pure vision to life. The Universal Peace Sanctuary will honor Queen Mayadevi, who, with unconditional love, sacrificed her life and gave birth to Prince Siddhartha.

For over 2,500 years, Lumbini has been an important pilgrimage destination; however, for centuries, it was largely overlooked. In 1967, U Thant, Secretary-General of the United Nations, visited Lumbini, Nepal, and was deeply inspired by its profound significance. He suggested developing Lumbini into an international center for peace. The United Nations commissioned the renowned Japanese architect Kenzo Tange to develop a master plan for the site, which was completed in 1978.

In 1985, the Lumbini Development Trust was established to implement the master plan, which included two designated zones for monasteries. The first monastery was built in 1992, and many more have been constructed since then. In 2012, the Lumbini Development Trust sought a custodian to develop a parcel of land and build a monastery adjacent to the Sacred Garden, the birthplace of Prince Siddhartha.

Around this time, His Eminence published and launched a Nepali translation of his first book, *Living Fully: Finding Joy in Every Breath*, in Kathmandu. This event raised awareness of Rinpoche's teachings and activities in Nepal. Prominent business and community leaders suggested that Rinpoche's non-profit organization, Rangrig Yeshe, Inc. USA, apply for stewardship of the land. They sincerely believed that Rinpoche would be an excellent representative for peace in the 21st century, and Rinpoche graciously agreed to their request. As a result, Rangrig Yeshe, Inc. was awarded a 99-year lease on the land. His Eminence was entrusted with constructing a peace sanctuary in Lumbini.

The Universal Peace Sanctuary, Rendering by K plus K Associates, Hong Kong

Fortuitous events brought Rinpoche together with the prominent German architect, Professor Stephan Braunfels. During their first meeting, the professor kindly offered to assist Rinpoche in designing and collaborating on a monastery project. As Rinpoche was applying for a permit to lease the land, he received a message from Braunfels inquiring about the plans for the monastery project they had previously discussed. Rinpoche mentioned that there could be a significant project on the horizon. When the lease on the land was nearing completion, Shyalpa Rinpoche and the professor traveled to Lumbini to survey the site. They were both excited about the project and began collaborating on a design for the Universal Peace Sanctuary.

Rinpoche envisions a sanctuary of spiritual refuge that transcends the limiting boundaries of religion, culture, race, and nationality. As all beings seek happiness and relief from suffering, they stand as equal partners in their quest for inner peace and fulfillment. The Universal Peace Sanctuary will honor Queen Mayadevi, who gave birth to Prince Siddhartha, and all mothers who exemplify selfless love in nurturing their children. Unconditional love is the wellspring of peace in the world.

Rinpoche invites everyone to support this sacred project with their positive intentions, talents, ingenuity, or a single contribution of at least one dollar, yuan, or euro. The sanctuary's purpose is to nurture seeds of universal harmony and peace. Everyone is encouraged to participate with a pure and generous heart, free from personal agendas. Rinpoche encourages everyone to become stakeholders in this historic peace project. It is everyone's responsibility to support world peace through cultivating inner peace. Anyone inspired to contribute is invited by Rinpoche to be creative and share their assistance, skills, and resources.

The Universal Peace Forum

The Universal Peace Forum was successfully launched at the World Economic Forum in Davos, Switzerland, on January 21, 2025. This initiative marks a transformative moment in our collective efforts to promote a more harmonious world, highlighting the connection between inner peace and global peace.

The World Economic Forum, known for promoting dialogue and collaboration, was the birthplace of the Universal Peace Forum. This platform aims to bring together individuals, organizations, and nations in a shared pursuit of peace. The Universal Peace Forum will be formed as a nonprofit charitable organization, initially headquartered in Geneva, where the Universal Peace Sanctuary Foundation is currently registered. Rinpoche envisions establishing Universal Peace Forum chapters in countries around the world.

The Universal Peace Forum aspires to "make peace more fashionable than war," a legacy we can proudly pass on to future generations. The historic launch of the Universal Peace Forum in Davos reminds us of our duty to uphold peace as a fundamental right and to embrace human rights as a collective responsibility. The Universal Peace Forum and the Universal Peace Sanctuary will support each other as two sides of the same coin.

Shyalpa Tenzin Rinpoche views the Universal Peace Forum in Davos as a complementary influence to the world's economic and technological progress—a "software of peace" that promotes ongoing dialogue among leaders from various fields, in conjunction with the Universal Peace Sanctuary. This unique assembly will bring together individuals who are wholeheartedly dedicated to harmonious interaction, merging ancient wisdom, modern innovation, and compassionate leadership to achieve world peace through inner peace.

Rinpoche says, "In our pursuit of material wealth and progress, many have forgotten how to celebrate the richness of life itself." The Universal Peace Forum seeks to weave a luminous thread of unity through the fabric of our shared humanity, inspiring individuals to rediscover their innate capacity for freedom, independence, and boundless joy.

As global economic leaders gather in Davos to address the forces shaping our future, the Universal Peace Forum initiative serves as a powerful guide and reminder that progress is measured not merely by material wealth but by the depth of our shared connections. Compassionate energy allows us to celebrate our lives and skillfully enjoy the benefits of material success. The Universal Peace Forum will contribute to a more peaceful and prosperous future for all beings.

GLOSSARY

Amitayus (Tib. *Tsepame*). Amitayus means "Boundless Infinite Life." In this context, Amitayus is a dharmakaya Buddha. Typically, Amitayus is usually depicted as red without a consort. However, in the *Pema Sangtig Ngondro*, Amitayus is white and shown with a consort.

as it is (Tib. *rang sor*). The freshness of one's original natural state.

awareness (Tib. *rigpa*). In ordinary usage, it denotes the insightful awareness of ordinary people. In Dzogchen, it refers to enlightened awareness of things as they are.

bell and vajra. The bell (Tib. *drilbu*) and vajra (Tib. *dorje*) form a pair, representing two aspects of a single unity. The bell in the left hand symbolizes the feminine principle of emptiness or wisdom, while the vajra, held in the right hand, corresponds to the masculine principle of skillful means or compassion. Emptiness and skillful means are primarily associated with the mahayana tradition and constitute two aspects of one unity. Their manifestations are wisdom and compassion. Dorje (*vajra*) translates as "Lord of Stones," thus meaning diamond-like or indestructible.

bodhichitta (Tib. *jang chub kyi sem*). The mind of enlightenment. On the relative level, it is the wish to guide sentient beings to enlightenment. To generate bodhichitta, one trains in various practices, such as the four immeasurables and the six paramitas. On the absolute level, bodhicitta is direct insight into the emptiness of self and phenomena.

bodhisattva. A being in whom bodhichitta arises effortlessly and who is devoted to the cultivation of the six perfections in order to attain enlightenment for the welfare of all beings.

body, speech, and mind. The "three doors" through which one enters and practices the path. The three doors are often correlated with the three kayas, nirmanakaya, sambhogakaya, and dharmakaya, and with the three seed syllables OM, AH, and HUM.

buddha (Tib. *sangye*). The Tibetan term consists of two words: awake and expanding. Purifying dark ignorance and obscuration, one is awakened. "Expanding," or "blossoming," refers to the limitless positive qualities of enlightenment within the realization of emptiness.

buddha nature. The potential within all sentient beings to realize the enlightenment of a buddha—the ultimate level of compassion and wisdom, beyond all limitations and boundaries.

Chatral Sangye Dorje Rinpoche. A Tibetan Dzogchen master and reclusive yogi, known for his profound realization and strict discipline. Chatral Sangye Dorje was a disciple of Khenpo Ngawang Pelzang and was widely regarded as one of the most highly realized Dzogchen yogis. In addition to his relationship with Khenpo Ngagchung, Chatral Sangye Dorje also studied with some of the last century's most renowned masters, including Dudjom Jigdral Yeshe Dorje, Dzongsar Khyentse Chökyi Lodrö, and the famed Kunzang Dekyong Wangmo. Chatral Sangye Dorje was one of the primary lineage holders of the Longchen Nyingthig, particularly the lineage that descends through Jigme Lingpa's heart son, Jigme Gyalwe Nyugu, and then on to Patrul Rinpoche. His Holiness Chatral Rinpoche was Shyalpa Tenzin Rinpoche's root teacher.

compassion. Compassion for all beings is a distinguishing feature of the great vehicle, the mahayana. In Dzogchen, compassion is equivalent to the power of manifestation, the form kayas (rupakaya), which provides benefit for others, and dharmakaya, benefit for oneself. In Dzogchen, bodhicitta is the absolute mind of enlightenment, equivalent to pure awareness, rigpa. Within that, nothing faulty and nothing dualistic exists.

complete settling/resting. The meditative practice of integration into natural, uncontrived resting of body and mind, rather than artificial concentration through action and effort.

conceptualization (Tib. *togpa*). Refers to understanding things through concepts. From the Dzogchen perspective, conceptual statements may be valid in a relative sense, yet they are empty of absolute truth. In Dzogchen, the direct experience of seeing things as they truly are goes beyond conceptualization.

cyclic existence. Taking uncontrolled rebirth under the influence of defilement and karmic imprints. The process arises from ignorance and is marked by suffering.

daka (Tib. *pawo*). Spiritual heroes or warriors, or celestial "sky-goers." They serve as the masculine counterparts of dakinis and are tantric deities who protect and uphold the Dharma.

dakini (Tib. *khandro*). Literally, a lady who dances in the sky. Usually, a dakini refers to a female tantric deity of the five families who guards, serves, presents, and embodies the tantric teachings and is a consort of a male tantric deity. They symbolize compassion, emptiness, and wisdom; the basic fertile space from which everything arises; and the tricky and playful aspects of empty phenomena.

Dharma (Skt.), (Tib. *cho.*). The term has many meanings. The most relevant are: 1. Dharma (capitalized), the buddhadharma, usually means the teachings of Buddha. In Dzogchen, the vision of realization is called "the Dharma." If the Guru transmits this vision, it is called "giving the Dharma." 2. Dharma (not capitalized), phenomena knowable by the mind, whether or not they are known as they really are.

dharmadhatu (Tib.) *choying*. Space, source, or realm of phenomena.

Dudjom Rinpoche/Dudjom Jikdral Yeshe Dorje (1904-1987). One of Tibet's foremost yogins, scholars, and meditation masters. He was recognized as the incarnation of Dudjom Lingpa (1835-1904), whose previous incarnations included the greatest masters, yogins, and punditas, such as Shariputra, Saraha, and Khye'u

Chung Lotsawa. Considered the living representative of Padmasambhava, he was a great revealer of the "treasures" (terma) concealed by Padmasambhava. A prolific author and meticulous scholar, Dudjom Rinpoche wrote more than forty volumes, one of the best known being his monumental work, *The Nyingma School of Tibetan Buddhism: Its Fundamentals and History.* In the last decade of his life, he spent much time teaching in the West, where he helped establish the Nyingma tradition, founding major centers in France and the United States.

Dzogchen. Translates to Great Perfection or Great Completeness. This teaching represents the pinnacle of the Tibetan Nyingma tradition. It is transmitted from the primordial Buddha Samantabhadra (*Kuntuzangpo*, Tib.) through the sambhogakaya Vajrasattva to the first human master in India, Garab Dorje. From Garab Dorje, the lineage was transmitted to the self-arisen Buddha Padmasambhava (Guru Rinpoche), who brought it to Tibet.

Dzogchen is the self-perfected state of our primordial nature, already complete from the beginningless beginning. It is uncreated and spontaneously accomplished. The precious Guru introduces us to this view, which is then stabilized in meditation. Thus, in this path, the result is itself the path.

elaboration. The generation of conceptual thoughts and conceptualized phenomena. The complexity of one's mental continuum increases as one generates an overwhelming multiplicity of discursive thoughts. Elaboration also refers to the fragmentation of the original unity of the Great Perfection into a delusive variety of separate entities believed to exist independently from the mind, each with its own real nature.

empowerment. The conferring of power or authorization to practice certain vajrayana teachings, the indispensable entrance door to tantric practice. Empowerment gives control over one's vajra body, vajra speech, and vajra mind and confers the ability to regard forms as deity, sounds as mantra, and thoughts as wisdom.

emptiness (Skt.) shunyata. The absence of inherent existence in all phenomena was explained by the Buddha in the sutras of t he second turning of the Wheel of Dharma and further elaborated upon by masters such as Nagarjuna and Chandrakirti. Emptiness is the lack of inherent existence of one's own nature or the nature of any phenomenon or person. The six elements are intrinsically empty. They are not real. The past, present, and future cannot be held or possessed. What happened in the past is not real since it has already passed. The present is also false because it becomes the past as soon as it appears. The future has not even come yet, so it, too, is empty of inherent existence.

energy, power, potential (Tib.) *tsal.* As a Dzogchen term, energy is the mind's intrinsic power to give rise to luminous manifestation that does not depart from its essence, emptiness. Jigme Lingpa said: "phenomena have arisen as the play of the energy of the mind." Thus, for example, the sun and its rays are regarded as changelessly pure but capable of being concealed by the play of obscuring clouds. Longchenpa says, "The essence of awareness is like a mirror. Its energy is like the clarity of the mirror. From this clarity, the play of manifestation arises like reflections in the mirror. When this manifestation arises, it does not move from the essence of mind, dharmakaya. So this manifestation is also dharmakaya."

essence. The inherent or unchanging nature of a thing or class of things.

five poisons/afflictions. The five afflictive emotions are attachment, aversion, ignorance, pride, and jealousy.

five primordial wisdoms. Mirror-like wisdom, wisdom of equality, discriminative wisdom, all-accomplishing wisdom, and wisdom of all-pervading space.

four boundless qualities or four immeasurables. 1) boundless lovingkindness (Skt. *maitri*, Tib. *jampa*), 2) boundless compassion (Skt. *karuna*, Tib. *nyingje*), 3) boundless joy (Skt. *mudita*, Tib. *gawa*), and 4) boundless equanimity (Skt. *upeksa*, Tib. *tang nyom*). One engages in these four practices with the thought of directing them toward and sharing them with all sentient beings.

four self-empowerments (Tib. *wang zhi*). In Guru Yoga, one practices the four self-empowerments. They are termed self-empowerments because they are achieved through one's visualization and understanding of the practice. It is important to engage in this practice regularly, if possible, daily, to repair and renew broken *samaya* and purify the consequences of the ten non-virtuous actions and the obscurations of one's three doors. The four empowerments are:

The vase empowerment (Tib. *bum wang*). With this empowerment, one visualizes the crystal white letter OM at the Guru's forehead, sending rays of white light to one's own forehead. Through this, the non-virtues and obscurations of the body, as well as the defects of the channels, are purified. One receives the blessing of the vajra body, is empowered in the practice of visualization, and the seed is planted to attain the nirmanakaya.

The secret empowerment (Tib. *sang wang*). With this empowerment, one visualizes the ruby red letter AH at the throat center of the Guru. Red light descends like lightning to one's throat center. Through this, negative acts of speech, as well as the winds in the body, are purified. One receives the blessing of vajra speech, becomes empowered in the practice of the channels and energies, and mantra recitation, planting the seed to attain the sambhogakaya body.

The wisdom empowerment (Tib. *sherab kyi wang*). One visualizes a sapphire-blue letter HUM at the heart of the Guru. Dark blue light comes from the Guru's heart to one's heart center, purifying all non-virtue and obscurations of the mind. One's creative essence or energy is purified, one receives the blessing of vajra mind, and the seed is planted to attain the dharmakaya body.

The Word Empowerment (Tib: *tshig wang*). One visualizes rays of light in five colors (white, red, blue, yellow, and green) emanating from the Guru's navel center. This light dissolves into one's navel center, purifying all subtle defilements and obscurations arising from the universal ground (Skt. *alaya vijnana*). One receives the blessing of vajra wisdom, is empowered to meditate on the natural Great Perfection (Dzogchen), and the seed is planted for attaining the state of the "spontaneously accomplished vidyadhara" (awareness holder).

grasper and grasped/apprehender and apprehended. The fixating, grasping mind and the fixated, grasped object. Both are illusory, samsaric fixations postulating independent, truly existing subjects and objects. The true, enlightened object is the three kayas, emptiness possessing all the supreme aspects. The true, enlightened subject is awareness, primordial wisdom. They are inseparable, non-dual self-insight.

great accomplishment (Skt. *siddhi*). The ordinary accomplishments are various miraculous abilities, such as knowing the minds of others. The supreme siddhi is enlightenment.

great equanimity. All phenomena are equal in not going beyond the essence of phenomena, which is emptiness inseparable from awareness. Since everything is equally the complete fulfillment, or great bliss, of enlightenment, the experience of enlightened beings has the quality of great equanimity.

Great Perfection. (see Dzogchen)

hinayana. The vehicle of individual liberation that practices to attain the fruits of sravakayana and pratyekabuddhayana but does not aim for the complete enlightenment of a Buddha.

hooked knife and skull cup. The hooked knife has a blade shaped like a half-moon, a hook on one end, and a vajra-topped handle. It symbolizes severing the root of attachment. The skull cup filled with blood represents the life force of compassion.

ignorance (Tib. *marigpa*). The cognitive inability to perceive things as they are, in contrast to rigpa, pristine awareness. This duality of grasper and grasped obscures knowledge. Furthermore, ignorance (Tib. *ti mug*) is an afflictive emotion, one of the three defiling poisons, along with attachment and aversion.

illusion. Examples of illusion are the moon's reflection in the water, optical illusion, mirage, dream, echo, city of the Gandharvas, hallucination, rainbow, lightning, bubbles on water, and reflection in the mirror.

indefinite, uncertain, unpredictable. In ordinary thought and experience, uncertainty usually has a negative connotation. However, in Dzogchen, the connotation is often positive, referring to freedom from conceptual restriction in enlightened experience.

indestructible (Tib. *jig med, dorje*, Skt. *vajra*). The essence of phenomena, emptiness, is changeless and thus uncreated and indestructible. In Dzogchen, when this is realized as one's true nature, one is said to gain the indestructible vajra body.

in its own place (Tib. *rang sar*). Naturally, spontaneously, in its own way; in itself; as it is.

Jigme Lingpa. A Tibetan terton of the Nyingma lineage of Tibetan Buddhism. He promulgated the Longchen Nyingthig, the Heart Essence teachings of Longchenpa, from whom, according to tradition, he received a vision in which the teachings were revealed. The Longchen Nyingthig eventually became the most famous and widely practiced cycle of Dzogchen teachings. His Eminence Shyalpa Rinpoche's main lineage practice is the Longchen Nyingthig.

karma. Habitual patterns of dualistic grasper and grasped, and the resulting afflictions of the five poisons, which ceaselessly accumulate in the continuum of a sentient being and determine future experiences through their power. Since the causality of karmic seeds in beings' continuums persists even after death, karma influences the circumstances of a being's rebirths across the various realms of samsara.

Lama (Tib). Lama can refer to any monk. References to "the Lama," particularly when capitalized, denote a realized teacher of the vajrayana. In this context, the term is synonymous with Guru (Skt.).

lotus flower. A symbol of purity. The lotus grows in muddy water, but blooms unstained and unsullied by the mud. Thus, it is an analogy for buddha nature or the true nature of mind. Guru Rinpoche was born fully formed as an eight-year-old boy in the heart of a lotus flower, demonstrating his pure and undefiled nature. Therefore, he is also known as the Lotus-Born (Tib. *Pema Jugne*, Skt. *Padmakara*).

Lotus-Born. See lotus flower

Longchenpa/Longchen Rabjam Drime Ozer. A Tibetan scholar-yogi of the Nyingma school and one of the most brilliant teachers in the Nyingma lineage. He systematized the Nyingma teachings in his *Seven Treasures* and wrote extensively on Dzogchen. He transmitted the Longchen Nyingtik cycle of teachings and practices to Jigme Lingpa, which has since become one of the most widely practiced traditions. Longchenpa was also a *terton* (treasure revealer), and some of his works, like the Khadro Yangtig, are considered *terma* (revealed treasure texts). Longchenpa's collection of over 270 texts encapsulates the core of the Nyingma Lineage, and is a critical link between the school's exoteric (sutra) and esoteric (tantric) teachings.

luminous/luminously clear (Tib.) *osel*. The phenomena of enlightened awareness are said to be empty in essence and luminously clear by nature.

magic show. In Dzogchen, since all that appears is empty of inherent existence, appearances resemble the magical display of illusory horses, elephants, and so forth conjured by a magician.

mahayana (Skt.). The "Great Vehicle," by which one proceeds to the state of perfect enlightenment of a buddha.

mandala offering. A practice that combines meditation, mantra, purification, and offerings into one powerful act. Many teachers recommend this practice as an essential daily ritual since it purifies negative karma and accumulates merit for ourselves and all beings.

mantra (Skt.). A syllable or series of syllables recited with magical effect, such as OM MANI PADME HUM. Included are seed syllables used to invoke deities.

Milarepa. (circa 1052 – circa 1135 CE) A Tibetan Buddhist yogi, a disciple of Marpa Lotsawa, and an important figure in the Kagyu lineage. He is widely regarded as one of Tibet's most revered yogis and poets.

mind. 1. mind in general (Tib.) *sem* (neutral sense). 2. dualistic mind (pejorative sense). 3. The nature of mind itself, bodhicitta (Tib.) *sem nyi* (positive sense).

moon disk. A symbol of a deity not stained by impurity. In representing a wisdom deity or enlightened being, the deity sits on a moon disc, which rests upon a lotus flower.

natural place, own place (Tib. *rang sa*). Phenomena are said to be in their own or proper place when experienced as they truly are—empty, luminous, and unceasing. Sometimes, emotions are considered to be in their proper place when directed toward the right objects. Ordinary dualistic passion, anger, and pride directed at others are afflictive emotions. Passion for enlightenment and a virtuous life, sadness over the suffering caused by ignorance and delusion, and pride in having the nature of the deity are referred to as the corresponding vajra emotions and are regarded as excellent virtues.

natural state. As it is, naturalness, natural flow, spontaneous, naturally occurring. These are synonymous with the Great Perfection.

nature of phenomena (Tib. *chonyi*, Skt. *dharmata*). The nature of phenomena is emptiness, so in phenomenal space (*dharmadhatu*), the true nature of phenomena (*dharmata*) is what is seen. In Dzogchen, this is the great emptiness beyond conceptualization, things as they are.

ngondro (Tib.). meaning "preliminary" or "that which goes first."

nirmanakaya (Skt.). The "body of manifestation" is that aspect that manifests out of compassion for the sake of sentient beings. The nirmanakaya could be said to emanate from the sambhogakaya.

non-duality. The non-existence of grasper and grasped. The grasper is the perceiver of samsara, while the grasped is the delusory object. They are misperceived as separate entities, leading to a dualistic view. Neither the grasper nor the grasped possesses inherent existence.

obscurations (Tib. *dippa*). Refers to two main types of hindrances: cognitive obscurations and emotional obscurations. Cognitive obscurations involve the dualistic perception of grasper and grasped, while emotional obscurations lead to attachment and aversion. These obscurations are the primary obstacles to achieving omniscience and experiencing a pure mind characterized by non-dual luminous clarity. In this non-dual state, one transcends karma and suffering.

OM AH HUM (Skt.). The three seed syllables correspond to the three doors of body, speech, and mind. They represent the three kayas—nirmanakaya, sambhogakaya, and dharmakaya.

outer, inner, and secret. Outer concerns the external world, inner concerns the body, and secret concerns the inner life of thoughts, feelings, etc.

Padmasambhava (Skt.). Also known as Guru Rinpoche and *Pema Jungney* (Lotus Born). Revered as the second Buddha, he established the Dzogchen teachings in Tibet. The Dharma King Trisong Deutsen invited Padmasambhava at the urging of

Abbot Shantarakshita to subdue and tame hostile forces in the Himalayan region.

Padmasambhava made many predictions, blessed many artifacts, and gave numerous teachings and practices, all of which were concealed with the assistance of his consort, Yeshe Tsogyal, with the intent that they be revealed in the future when the time was right for their discovery and propagation. These hidden and later revealed or rediscovered "treasures" are called *terma*. The Padma Sangtig cycle of texts and teachings is *terma*, revealed by the *terton*, Kyabgon Jedrung Rinpoche, Dudjom Namkhai Dorje.

As we practice, we regard our teachers and Gurus not only as representatives of Guru Rinpoche, who is no different in essence from Lord Buddha, but also as Guru Rinpoche himself. In a sense, one might say, using the terminology of Western psychology, that Guru Rinpoche is the archetypal Guru.

Paramitas. The six perfections of generosity, ethical discipline, patience, diligence, meditation, and wisdom utilized for self-cultivation on the bodhisattva path to buddhahood.

Patrul Rinpoche. One of the greatest Nyingma teachers of the nineteenth century, respected by all traditions in Tibet. He taught extensively on bodhicitta and Shantideva's *Bodhisattvacharyavatara* (A Guide to the Bodhisattva's Way of Life). Most Nyingma teachers today trace their lineage through him. Patrul Rinpoche's *Kunzang Lama'i Zhalung*, translated as The Words of My Perfect Teacher, is considered the definitive commentary on the Longchen Nyingtig Ngondro and an excellent commentary for Nyingma ngondro in general. It is essential reading for any serious practitioner. Patrul Rinpoche wrote this work based on oral commentary and guidance from his root teacher, Jigme Gyalwai Nyugu, who received it from his root teacher, the great Jigme Lingpa. (see Jigme Lingpa)

Pema Sangtig Ngondro (Tib.) Meaning "Secret Essence of Padmasambhava." It is the name for the entire cycle of texts discovered and taught by the *terton*, Kyabgon Jedrung Rinpoche, Dudjom Namkhai Dorje, the root Teacher of H.H. Taklung Shabdrung Rinpoche. Taklung Shabdrung Rinpoche transmitted this precious tradition to H.E. Shyalpa Tenzin Rinpoche.

primordially pure. Since the essence of the Great Perfection is emptiness, it is always pure of all defilements and clear of all obscurations.

rigpa (Skt. *vidya*). Generally, it means "intelligence" or "awareness." However, in Dzogchen, the highest teachings of the Buddhist tradition in Tibet, rigpa carries a more profound meaning: the innermost nature of mind itself. The entirety of the Buddha's teachings directs us toward realizing the ultimate quality of rigpa, the state of enlightenment.

samadhi (Skt.). Meditation, but more specifically, undistracted concentration or meditative absorption. It literally means "adhering to continuity or evenness.

Samantabhadra (Skt.). In the Nyingma, the "old" or original translation school established in Tibet by Padmasambhava, the dharmakaya is typically represented by the primordial Buddha Samantabhadra (Tib. *Kuntuzangpo*), who is dark blue and naked, in union with his consort Samantabhadri (Tib. *Kuntuzangmo*). This represents the inseparable union of awareness and emptiness, as well as the pure, absolute nature that is always present and unobstructed. In the Sarma, the "new" translation school traditions, the dharmakaya is usually represented by Vajradhara (Tib: *Dorje Chang*).

samaya (Skt.). In the Vajrayana, it refers to the conduct required of a tantric practitioner, outlined in a set of vows or commitments. Samaya represents a sacred bond between the Guru and disciple.

sambhogakaya. The "body of perfect enjoyment" is the spontaneously luminous aspect of Buddhahood, perceptible only to highly realized beings. It can be seen as a reflection of the dharmakaya. The sambhogakaya is typically depicted in elaborately and richly ornamented forms. It is transmitted from mind to mind. Examples of wisdom deities shown in sambhogakaya form include Vajrasattva, Manjushri, Avalokitesvara, Vajrapani, Tara, and others.

same taste (Tib. *ron yam*). The inherent purity and empty nature of all phenomena. A realized being resting in the state of same taste is beyond clinging to dualistic concepts, such as good and bad, desirable and undesirable, etc.

samsara (Skt.). Samsara can be translated as "suffering cyclic existence." This encompasses all six realms of rebirth. The Tibetan word is *khorwa*, which literally means cycle.

Shakyamuni Buddha. The historical Buddha of our time. Born as Prince Siddhartha Gautama, Shakyamuni means "sage of the Shakyas." Shakya was the family name of Lord Buddha.

six realms. The god realm, jealous god realm, human realm, animal realm, hungry ghost realm, and hell realm. The first three represent higher realms, resulting from positive karma, while the last three constitute lower realms, stemming from negative karma.

spontaneously accomplished (Tib. *lhundrub*). Self-existing. Having the sense of something that is naturally so and does not need to be created or contrived.

sun disk. Symbolizes freedom from all impurities.

ten virtues. Renunciation of the ten non-virtues: 1. Not destroying life. 2. Not stealing. 3. Refraining from improper sexual activity. 4. Not telling lies. 5. Not using abusive language. 6. Not slandering others. 7. Not indulging in meaningless speech. 8. Not being covetous. 9. Not being malicious. 10. Not holding wrong beliefs.

Three Jewels/Triple Gem. The Buddha, Dharma, and Sangha are collectively known as the Three Jewels or the Triple Gem (Tib: *kun chok sum*). The Guru's body, speech, and mind embody the Three Jewels.

three poisons. Attachment, aversion, and ignorance. These are the three root defilements that create samsara. An accomplished yogi is free of them.

three realms. The desire realm, form realm, and formless realm. None of these realms transcends samsara.

The desire realm encompasses hell beings, hungry ghosts, animals, humans, jealous gods, and god realm. Also included within the god realm are the form realms and formless realms.

The form realm consists of four levels of meditative absorption, where the fulfillment of desire is attained.

The formless realm includes four states inhabited by gods without bodily forms, existing in states of absorption. Because they lack physical form, they cannot hear the Dharma. The fourth formless absorption is the cause of rebirth within the peak of cyclic existence, the highest level of existence within samsara.

three roots (Tib: *tsa sum*). The Lama, Yidam, and Dakini are collectively referred to as the three roots. The Lama serves as the root or source of blessings; the Yidam is the source of accomplishments, and the Dakini is the source of activities. A Yidam is a wisdom deity, peaceful or wrathful, that one meditates upon. The Dakini, or khandro (Tib.), embodies the feminine principle associated with wisdom. This term encompasses many types of dakinis and various levels of meaning.

three types of suffering. 1. the suffering of suffering, 2. the suffering of change, 3. all-pervasive suffering of conditioned existence.

togal (tib.). *Togal* is the practice of the direct perception of pristine consciousness and is translated as "direct crossing" or "leapover." This practice can quickly lead to the actual realization of the three kayas in this lifetime, and thus is a more rapid way of bringing about the dissolution of the practitioner's karmic vision. The practice of *togal* brings the realization of "spontaneous presence (*lhundrup*), and it can only be undertaken by one who has first gained stability in the practice of *trekchod,* with the guidance of a Dzogchen master.

trekchod (tib.). *Trekchod* means "cutting of tension" or "cutting through solidity." In this practice, one first identifies and then sustains recognition of one's own innately pristine, empty awareness. *Trekchod* is instant freshness, unspoiled by the thoughts of the three times that one directly sees in actuality by letting be in naturalness.

true nature/innate nature. The enlightened nature, beyond all confusion and obscuration. It is innate in all beings; therefore, all beings have the potential to attain enlightenment.

two accumulations. The accumulation of merit and primordial wisdom. When they are complete, enlightenment and realization of the Great Perfection are realized.

unobstructed (Tib. *thog med*). In Dzogchen, it means unhindered and unceasing.

vajra (Tib. *dorje*). 1. The diamond, prince of stones. 2. Indestructible, adamantine. 3. The thunderbolt, the weapon of Indra.

Vajradhara (Skt.). In the *Pema Sangtig Ngondro*, the primordial dharmakaya Buddha is Vajradhara, representing the empty, uncompounded nature of mind. Vajradhara is dark blue, seated in the lotus posture, and holding a vajra and bell with his two hands crossed in front of his chest.

Vajrasattva (Tib: *Dorje Sempa*). Vajrasattva, which means "Indestructible Wisdom Being," is the sambhogakaya Buddha who transmitted the lineage to the first human Dzogchen teacher, Garab Dorje. Vajrasattva is white in color and highly ornamented with necklaces, armlets, bracelets, and beautiful robes. He sits in the vajra posture, united with his consort, holding a bell in his left hand at his hip and a *dorje* in his right hand at his heart. Sometimes, Vajrasattva is depicted without a consort. The practices of Vajrasattva meditation and mantra recitation primarily focus on purification and confession of wrongdoing.

vajrayana (Skt.). The vehicle of esoteric Buddhist teachings and practices aimed at bringing one swiftly to the state of enlightenment.

wisdom (Tib. *yeshe*). Literally, pristine or primordial awareness, knowledge, or cognition. Direct intuition of absolute reality, the intrinsic nature of mind.

H.E. SHYALPA TENZIN RINPOCHE

for more information visit:

PeaceSanctuary.org

Buddhafield.us

WenchengGongzhu.org

www.ingramcontent.com/pod-product-compliance
Lightning Source LLC
LaVergne TN
LVHW090602110826
845146LV00001B/232